PRAISE FOR

I WILL NOT GO

TRANSLATIONS, TRANSFORMATIONS & CHUTNEY FRACTALS

Mohabir modestly calls his project an "experiment"—it is a bold achievement documenting how this language, with its history of attempted annihilation, has managed to survive, evolve, migrate, and keep on singing.

— **R. ZAMORA LINMARK,** author of *Rolling the Rs*
and *The Importance of Being Wilde at Heart*

The inventive translations of chutney lyrics by these Caribbean writers collectively creates an intricate and many-layered sonic experience. But even more profound is the way in which by exploring the lyrics via multiple lenses, the voices and troubled experiences of Indo-Caribbean women are excavated and released—entwined, but also, hauntingly distinct from the high spirit of chutney beat. The result is powerful and very moving.

— **MARCIA DOUGLAS,** author of *The Marvellous
Equations of the Dread: A Novel in Bass Riddim*

[This book] is vital, and genius—chutney music as a source, creatively translated into a variety of Indo-Caribbean Englishes, a cultural resource, a map of origins, and a proclamation of resilience and survival.

— **SHANI MOOTOO,** author of *Cereus Blooms at Night*
and *Polar Vortex*

I WILL NOT GO

TRANSLATIONS, TRANSFORMATIONS & CHUTNEY FRACTALS

—

Edited by Rajiv Mohabir

Distributed by D.A.P./Distributed Art Publishers // artbook.com (800) 388-BOOK
ISBN: 9781935717003
Library of Congress Control Number: 2024943238
Cover artwork by Renluka Maharaj
Book design by Rhea I (www.oddwaffling.com)

This publication is made possible by support from the USC Dana and David Dornsife College of Arts, Letters, and Sciences; and the USC Department of American Studies and Ethnicity. Special thanks to Stephen CuUnjieng and the Choi Chang Soo Foundation for their support of this work.

Additional funding was provided by generous contributions from: Tanzila Ahmed, Chitra Aiyar, Chantal Rei Alberto, Sasha Ali, Hari Alluri, Heidi Amin-Hong, Stine An, Akhila Ananth, Tiffany Babb, Manibha Banerjee, Neelanjana Banerjee, Terry Bequette, Hung Bui, Cari Campbell, Emiliana Chan, Susan Chan, Sam Chanse, Alexander Chee, Anelise Chen, Anita Chen, Dehua Chen, Jean Chen, Lisa Chen, Floyd Cheung, Jayne Cho, Jennifer Chou, Yvonne Chow, Caroline Chow, Elizabeth Clemants, Tuyet Cong Ton Nu, Herna Cruz, Timothy Daley, Lawrence-Minh Bui Davis, Glenda Denniston, Susannah Donahue, Taiyo Ebato, Irving Eng, Matthew Fargo, Peter Feng, Sia Figiel, Sesshu Foster, Sylvana Freyberg, Diane Fujii, Joseph Goetz, K A Hashimoto, Jean Ho, Ann Holler, Huy Hong, Jacqueline Hoyt, Lisa Hsia, Jonathan Hugo, Adria Imada, Susan Ito, Ashaki Jackson, Carren Jao, Mia Kang, Andrew Kebo, Vandana Khanna, Nidhi Khurana, Seema Khurana, Swati Khurana, Joonie Kim, Seonglim Kim, Gwendolyn Knight, Sabrina Ko, Timothy Ko, Robin Koda, Juliana Koo, Sun Hee Koo, Rika Koreeda, Emily Kuhlmann, Eileen Kurahashi, Paul Lai, Jenny Lam, Iris Law, Samantha Le, Catherine Lee, Helen Kim Lee, Hyunjung Lee, Marie Myung-Ok Lee, Stacy Lee, Whakyung Lee in memory of Sonya Choi Lee, KC Lehman, Edward Lin, Carleen Liu, Veronica Liu, Mimi Lok, Andrea Louie, Pauline Lu, Haline Ly, Abir Majumdar, Jason McCall, Sally McWilliams, Sean Miura, Faisal Mohyuddin, Greg Monaco, Russell Morse, Adam Muto, Wendy Lou Nakao, Jean Young Naylor, Kim Nguyen, Kathy Nguyen, Viet Thanh Nguyen, Vinh Nguyen, erin ninh, Dawn Oh, Julia Oh, Eric Ong, Tiffany Ong, Camille Patrao, Thuy Phan, Cheryline Prestolino, James Pumarada, Jhani Randhawa, Amarnath Ravva, Maria L Sandoval, Nitasha Sawhney, Carol Say, Andrew Shih, Brandon Shimoda, Luisa Smith, Roch Smith, Jungmi Son, daniela sow, Nancy Starbuck, Karen Su, Rachana Sukhadia, Robin Sukhadia, Rajen Sukhadia, Kelly Sutherland, Willie Tan, Zhen Teng, Wendy Tokuda, Frederick Tran, Monique Truong, Patricia Wakida, Dan S. Wang, Aviva Weiner, Duncan Williams, William Wong, Amelia Wu and Sachin Adarkar, Anita Wu and James Spicer, Stan Yogi, Kyung Yoon, Shinae Yoon, Mikoto Yoshida, Patricia Yun, and many others.

Kaya Press is also supported, in part, by the National Endowment for the Arts; the Los Angeles County Board of Supervisors through the Los Angeles County Arts Commission; the Community of Literary Magazines and Presses and the Literary Arts Emergency Fund; and the City of Los Angeles Department of Cultural Affairs.

I WILL NOT GO

TRANSLATIONS, TRANSFORMATIONS & CHUTNEY FRACTALS

—

Edited by Rajiv Mohabir

KAYA
PRESS

for abi-dis—for matti
for all with an ocean in their blood
for all who seek the poetry in
the music of the ancestors
for all who dance

TABLE OF CONTENTS

FASTEN YOUR VEIL: TRANSLATIONS

FRACTALS I: THE AFTERLIVES OF CHUTNEY

LIKE CHUTNEY MASALA

Hear me, na. Chutney music is the country my waist comes from. It needs no visa, no sponsorship. It burns in my hips and arms like a wild fire stoked from the ravages of a little-known history.

One of the great multimodal art forms of the Caribbean—alongside merengue, soca, calypso, and reggae—chutney music comes from North Indian folk music mixing with local black Caribbean song-ways, cultures, and languages. A nuanced and constantly evolving musical form, chutney also mirrors the history of our transformation from "indentured laborers" into Caribbean people.

Like the way my mother makes chutney of grated mango, ball of fiyah pepper, garlic, salt, and masalas, it's a condiment made from mixing: from Hindustani songs sung by the earliest laborers brought to British Guiana in 1938 to Sundar Popo's 1979 first album "Come Dance with the Champ" to Rikki Jai's 2005 release of "More-Tor", which brought chutney to a new generation of fans, to 21st-century artists like Drupatee.

I created this anthology to bring chutney poetics into a conversation about cultural production, transatlantic histories, and literature. The more people are able to read the poetry embedded in these songs and transformed by these poets—to understand the joys and horrors in the lyrics, available here in this anthology—the more chutney music will be seen for its poetic stakes and complex and nuanced radiance.

Coolie Arts and Poetics

After the British outlawed the international trade of enslaved people in 1834, they repurposed the mechanism of enslavement by indenturing over 1 million South Asians to work on sugarcane plantations run by them and other European colonies. We were called "Coolies"—the servants of Empire. We were given five-year renewable contracts and were promised a return home. But most of us never went back to what was then called India. Instead, we stayed and transformed Caribbean culture. The forms of art that sprung up from this displacement were relegated to the lower parts of society: namely music and public culture.

Coolie arts bring South Asian aural traditions into an acknowledgement of the violence of Transatlantic labor trajectories. Chutney music's lyrics of longing and loss tell the story of the harrowing ship journeys across the Kalapani, and the tortuous work of the cane fields. It also ties Coolie poetics to identity and labor economies. The canvas of the Caribbean continues to be colored by the legacy of plantations, dependency on rum as an escape from humiliation and domestic violence, and racial hierarches such as anti-Blackness and the settling of indigenous lands. Small wonder then that such themes play such a prominent part in the chutney songs of today.

Historically, Indo-Caribbean singers performed their compositions in Caribbean Hindustani, a koine language made up of a variety of South Asian languages such as Bhojpuri, Awadhi, Magahi, Maithili, Tamil, Bengali, and others. This complex mix of vernaculars was often referred to "broken Hindi."

Broken, broken, broken. This word cut my family deep. Broken: not the violent system that impoverished my family, just the culture they hailed from. And so broken we became—Hindustani drying up in my parents' throats.

Even today, there's a strong belief that the only books of value are those written in English.

This erasure perpetrated by Empire—one that hinges on the notion of the Coolie as a servile instrument of Empire, brown bodies lesser than human—makes clear the reason why this plantation language, specific to each Indian community in the Caribbean and complete with linguistic verve and dexterity, did not become a language to be written down.

Against Inscrutability

There's a frequent claim by White ethnomusicologists who study the musical form that chutney lyrics are inscrutable. They claim that Indians in the Caribbean cannot speak Hindi or Bhojpuri, so there's nothing worth considering in the lyrics of these song-poems, that they do not require any further study. In his article published in *Popular Music* in 1998, "Chutney and Indo-Trinidadian Cultural Identity," Peter Manuel states: "Chutney lyrics are semantically insignificant because of their conventionality and, more obviously, because of the fact that they are sung in a language (Bhojpuri Hindi) which is largely unintelligible to most Indo-Trinidadians and Guyanese." Such claims actively erase Indo-Caribbean experience and language use. They erase the fact that my Aji spoke this language.

In fact, most Indo-Caribbean people I know have access to translations of the gist of chutney lyrics through elders with whom they are close. Even before I began my own journey of studying Bhojpuri and Hindi, I always knew someone who could offer me a gloss or rough translation of whatever song I was singing along with or dancing to. The lyrics—though not translated word for word—were nevertheless important to how I understood myself and the place I come from.

The fact that these translations took place in this way is itself significant. It's an important form of Creolese gist-giving, one that offers more than just the words someone is singing. I remember my Aji telling me, in her distinct mix of Creole and Guyanese Bhojpuri, to stop singing "Chadar Bichao Balma" ("Spread the sheet, my beloved") in front of her because it was a "rude" song. "Langtime people been a besaram," she would say, sucking her teeth as she spoke. "People long ago were shameless." She would also request that same song to be played at family parties.

Chutney Fractals

This collection of translations and fractals of chutney music by multiple translators and writers is an experiment. Chutney music has been a kind of food to me, nourishing my poems and my poetic mind. Its themes of play, religion and myth, love and loss, have been instrumental in the ways I think of my own poems, the metaphors available to me as I write in a completely new national context in the United States.

I want to know what of chutney poetry survives the loss of language and derision. To this end, I've asked Caribbean writers and poets to "translate" the lyrics to two different songs, using their own diasporic voices. These writers speak from their own intersections and assemblages of identities (sexualities, ethnicities, religions, places of national origin, etc.), making possible a nuanced, migratory, shifting practice of poetics that breathes lexical fluidity back into the ways Coolie arts are practiced. Such a practice feels like spiritual kin to the jahaaji—the boat traveler—spirit of our ancestors.

It is also a response to my own experiences within the literary translation community in the United States, where the work of white translators are privileged and glorified over translators of color. When I first went to India to study Hindi and Bhojpuri on a language learning fellowship, my Guyanese pronunciations of certain words like belna and samundar were corrected by a woman on the program, the favorite of the Hindi teachers, while I was expected to know—inherently—a language my family never even spoke. The experience invoked a very old, familial trauma: *Am I even Indian?*

In graduate school, I once was shamed in a translation workshop for never having read Goethe, yet no one in that workshop had ever heard the names Babla and Kanchan. In the same class, we read Eliot Weinberger's anthology *19 Ways of Looking at Wang Wei*, which collects various translations and retranslations of Wang Wei's poem "Deer Park." Wei lived and wrote in China during the Tang Dynasty in the 7th Century, yet this volume collected the work of nineteen different translators engaging with Wei's poem with varying levels of Orientalism and ownership.

Being influenced to put this anthology together as a Caribbean, diasporic response to that text may seem reactionary, but in my mind it's spiritual. I am interested in asking Indo-Caribbean people how they interpret and live the templates of life found in these songs. Who—despite not knowing this language enough to speak it—were informed by their power. The investment feels ancestral; the songs a navel string that brings forth our bodies. If we don't translate these songs for ourselves now, who will? Someone who doesn't intimately know what it means to wine (THE chutney dance move that means *to wind your waist*)? Someone who has no idea what it feels like to go to a gay club in Toronto and hear Sonny Man's "Lotela" play on the speakers? So, this is personal. *I Will Not Go* seizes the reins back and puts our songs back in our mouths.

Ham Na Jaibe and Aaj Sawaliya

In *The Poem Behind the Poem: Translating Asian Poetry*, Arthur Sze gives a gloss of the Mandarin poetry that he translates, where each word is written in Chinese with its translation in English just under it. The effect is that the spread of words allows for readers to see exactly his process of migrating thoughts from one economized language into another system altogether. In using Arthur Sze's example, I show how complications in our oral culture work together to create an entirely new genre: the chutney song whose roots are in traditional Bhojpuri forms.

When thinking about songs that could represent my own sense of Caribbean acculturation, I was motivated by my own affective responses to two songs in particular. Both are playful and spiritual, but one is performed by someone with a Hindu name (Sundar Popo) and one is performed by someone with a Muslim name (Yusuff Khan). Together, these two singers show the diversity and flexibility in Caribbean performance.

Both Sundar Popo and Yusuff Khan are from Trinidad, and their music continues to be celebrated across the labor diaspora. I was particularly struck by one incident, in Kauaʻi, which I visited with my sister in 2005. There, in a town called Poipu, we met Fiji Indians who said they loved to dance to Sundar Popo at family functions. I was astonished to learn that these folks from the global South Asian labor diaspora outside of Guyana, Trinidad, Surinam, or Jamaica could be so intimately connected to our Caribbean culture. My ancestors could have stepped onto a different ship and ended up in the South Pacific working the cane fields of Fiji (or South Africa, Mauritius, or Réunion) and we still would wine to Popo and Khan. Meeting them was like looking into a mirror that revealed our chutneyed reflections.

The first song presented here is "Ham Na Jaibe," originally sung by Sundar Popo, regarded as one of the parents of chutney music. This song first appeared on the album *Come Dance With The Champ* (1979), which also features the hit songs "Phulauri Bina Chutney," "Nana and Nani," and "Scorpion Gyal." Popo is known for blending Hindustani and English in his lyrics, a reflection of the traditions of the music he originally learned. "Ham Na Jaibe" features a variety of Trinidadian Bhojpuri. The songs that Popo produced—particularly this one—often explore themes of leaving the natal home, for example after marriage. This major event, the switching of families, was often a traumatic one for the women coerced under patriarchal norms.

Domestic violence, alcohol dependency, and misogyny—major issues that our communities face—are rooted in the plantation economy and show up as symptoms of a certain kind of postcolonial disorder. "Ham Na Jaibe" highlights these issues and interactions. Chutney music, which developed out of songs sung by women for matikor rituals, also acted as instructions for women in homosocial spaces. What is real and what endures in Indo-Caribbean spaces is violence against women. Men continue to murder women like in the cases of Guiatree Hardat, Natasha Ramen, Donne Dojoy, Omwattie Fill, Riya Rajkumar, Rajwantie Baldeo, Stacy Singh, Vanessa Zaman, Christina Sukhdeo, and many others named by Caribbean Feminist Stories, Coolieween, the Jahajee Sisters.

The translators in this book show us how they are particularly haunted by these ghosts hiding in plain sight within the music. While not knowing the meaning "exactly," poet and writer Elizabeth Jaikaran writes in this book:

I've always found the vocalizations in chutney music to sound like lamentations, notwithstanding watching waistlines roll and hips pelt to their recitation . . . Reading the literal translations of these songs was sobering and eureka all at once.

The second song, "Aaj Sawaliya Sasur Ghar Jana," appears on an album released in 1980 called *Haunting Melodies of Yusuff Khan*. Although the name Yusuff Khan might appear to reflect a singer of Muslim heritage, to base such an assumption solely on a person's name would be to elide the complications of the Caribbean context: many of the "haunting melodies" Yusuff Khan sings are in fact Hindu devotional songs.

"Aaj Sawaliya Sasur Ghar Jana" is a case in point. The song's speaker mentions Kabir, one of the great bhakti devotional poets of India. The phrase "kehet Kabir" is Kabir's kavi-chhap, or signature, an indication that he is to be considered the author of this specific kind of poetry meant to be sung with the human voice. This literature, at least when it comes to Kabir's poems, relies on oral tradition for its revelations. A Muslim weaver who lived in the late 1400s and died in the 1500s, Kabir is said to have begun chanting the name of the Hindu deity Rama, who is not the Rama from the Ramayana, but rather the nirgun deity: the god without form. Kabir chanted in order to alleviate Maya, the grand illusion that the world consists of division and separation. The devotional aspect of this song—its queer potential, and its interreligious stakes—provides countless ways to enter this song-poem, multiplying and amplifying it in many directions.

Both of the songs I've chosen for this anthology pertain to leaving—a journey into the unknown, into diaspora. Be it a spiritual voyage to meet the Beloved without the veil or a journey into a new marital situation, these two songs speak to one another in our living rooms and on dancefloors across the entire world.

Translation in Motion

The writers included in these pages represent a new generational reckoning with chutney music. They include writers from the United States, the United Kingdom, Canada, Trinidad, and Guyana, with belongings also in Surinam and Jamaica. Consideration was also given to the diversity of gender identities, ethnicities, sexualities, and religious identities in our communities.

Since conceptions of grammar and diction in Caribbean Hindustani vary from community to community, and many of them do not speak either Bhojpuri or Caribbean Hindi fluently, I kicked off this project by providing each writer with a breakdown of each word's meaning. I then asked the writers to work through the songs themselves to carve out their own unique translation, according to their own specific idiom. Each writer was given the option to translate in Creolese, English, or any other Caribbean or local vernacular that they spoke or lived in.

Some writers chose to produce literal translations, some homophonic translations. Other writers opted to transpose, transfigure, and transform the original lyrics into pieces that fit their own poetic idioms. Krystal Ramroop chooses to indicate chorus and verse in her poem, which invokes the word "belna" to show its Caribbean feeling. Aliyah Khan, Nadia Misir, Nicholas Peters, and others write "direct translations" in Guyanese Creolese. These languages are, in a very powerful way, Asian American languages.

I was interested in learning about their affective and bodily responses to the songs throughout their lives, how we understand the music through our bones and lives, how our heart beats a chutney pulse. How the poetry lives inside us as our Ajis and Nanis—so I asked the writers to also contribute poetry inspired by the music itself.

As Kaneesha Cherelle Parsard writes in "The Coolie Woman Climbs Out of the Portrait," imaginative work enlivens the past and calls it forth into the present. Eddie Bruce-Jones in "Soon come" imagines the maintenance and evolution of food ways that have evolved in his Jamaican community. Alex Bacchus in "Kissmehass Rum Sukkah" unbinds the bound Coolie and uses the space to wine and to show the cultural diffusion of language from Kréyol, Spanish, and Creolese. Anita Baksh summons wedding time traditions and performs a subtle and poetic feminist critique through polyvocality.

After each translation and poem was completed, each writer wrote a short essay on their process and their own experiences with chutney music despite not knowing its language perfectly.

There are so many more manifestations of the chutney poetics to explore and discover in these writers' responses that every time I reencounter the work presented here, I learn something new about my diaspora and myself.

The chutney music I grew up with and have loved since before I could speak is a literature that is particular to my community—to my family. My father's parents were preliterate as were my mother's grandparents. Our literature as Guyanese Indians is the literature of that which is remembered and spoken. That which was chanted and sung in the cane fields while being punished by the unrelenting sun. That which was passed down from mother to daughter in the wedding house, used in ritual and for daily work.

The Caribbean is an infinitely creative space, transforming the cutlass and hoe of indenture into instruments, into song, into dance. Into chutney music. It moves in us as our heartbeats, breaks against the shore like Kalapani. Our musics themselves are syncretic, defining a culture that abi dis belong to: something mixed and new, birthed from the trauma of transoceanic passage and plantation, rooted in the wild dancing joy of our bodies.

May this anthology serve as a summoning, a collective invocation of our jahaaji ancestors. May it call down new ancestors into the coming generations.

Rajiv Mohabir
Denver, Colorado
October 2024

MY IN-LAW'S DOOR:

TRANSLATIONS

(Sundar Popo 1979)

Ham Nā Jāibe Sasur Ghar Mẽ Bābā

HAM	NĀ	JĀIBE	SASUR	GHAR	MẼ	BĀBA
I	no	will go	father-in-law	home	in	father

JIYARĀ	JAṚ	GAIL	HAMĀR	BĀBA
life	freeze	happened	my	father

Verse 1

ROJ ROJ	SASUR	DAṚŪ	PĪAT HE
daily daily	father-in-law	will go	is drinking

ROJ ROJ	SĀS	MORE	LAKṚI	KÕCAT HE
daily daily	mother-in-law	my	stick	is poking

Verse 2

ROJ ROJ	SĀS	MOR	CIJAWĀ	DIKHĀWE
daily daily	mother-in-law	my	things	shows

DEKHKE	SASUR	JIYĀ	LALCĀWE
having seen	father-in-law	life	greedy

Verse 3

SĀS	JHULĀWE	SĀSURWĀ	KE,	BĀBA
mother-in-law	makes swing	father-in-law	to	father

APNĪ	GODĪ	SAJARIYĀ	PE,	BĀBA
her	lap	adornment	on	father

Verse 3

SASUR	PĪTE	SASUIYĀ	KE	BĀBA
father-in-law	beats	mother-in-law	to	father

APNĪ	CHOTĪ	JHOPARIYĀ	MẼ	BĀBA
our	small	hut	in	father

SASUR	PĪTE	SASUIYĀ	KE	BĀBA
father-in-law	beats	mother-in-law	to	father

LEKE	APNI	LAKARIYĀ	SE	BĀBA
having taken	his	wood	with	father

Krystal M. Ramroop

I Will Not Go to My In-Laws Home

Chorus
I won't go to my in-laws home, papa.
My life will become hell, papa.

Verse 1
Every day father-in-law drinks alcohol.
Every day mother-in-law jabs me with her belna.

Verse 2
Mother-in-law displays her abundant possessions.
Father-in-law, enchanted, watches her hungrily with greed.

Verse 3
Mother-in-law rocks father-in-law like a baby.
His head decorates her lap as he sleeps his cares away.

Verse 4
Father-in-law beats mother-in-law, papa.
In our small home,
father-in-law beats mother-in-law viciously
with a tight grip on his cricket bat, papa.

Krystal M. Ramroop's other writings: 69, 85, 142

Aliyah Khan
Ah Cyah Go Da Man House

Me ain goin to dem people house Pa
Me life done stop Pa

He does drink rum whole day
She does beat me whole day

She always pasray pon de floor
He lele does drop when he see she

She does swing he to sleep
Wrap he up like pickney

But he does beat she Pa
Under the galvanize Pa
He does beat she Pa
Wid a big wood Pa

Me too Ma

Aliyah Khan's other writings: 56, 79, 126

Divya Persaud
I will not go

I won't go to my father-in-law's house,
baba, I won't be frozen there;

father:
I will not go to that man's place.

every day, he drinks,
and she prods me, every day.

every day, my things are hers:
his everyday greed.

> (he bejewels the hammock
> of her lap)

and in this small house he beats her:
he beats her with its wood

Divya Persaud's other writings: 54, 88, 104, 146

Kaneesha Cherelle Parsard
Old Day

I turn my back on my in-law's door

Days past, he'd turn to drink and she
to trouble me

Days past, she'd rouse him
they'd turn to one another

Later, she'd put him down
their embrace birthing stars

Another day would not be so sweet
He rises to beat her
and retires only when his arm tires

Kaneesha Cherelle Parsard's other writings: 61, 103, 155

Nadia Misir
na badda

na badda send me to he house,
baba. nah mek me punish suh.
whole day di man
gon knock he drink.
whole day he wife
gon knock me wit she stick.
whole day he tongue
ah hang out he mouth
when he wife ah pass.
is bareface he bareface,
baba. nah badda
send me to he house.
sas don' badda wid he,
she gon love he up

Nadia Misir's other writings: 70, 77, 144

Alex Bacchus
Meh Guh Stuck Deh So, Meh Nah Guh Go

Meh nah guh go
Meh nah guh go

Oh meh mamma
To faddahinla houws
Meh nah guh go

Meh nah guh go faddahinla houws
Cuz ayudeez nno meh guh stuhk deh so

Dayin ann dayowt, faddahinla a drink paiwari
Ann meh worry
Maan nah stahp suhk rum
Dayin ann dayowt, muddahinla a lash me bad so

Dayin ann dayowt, faddahinla wikked
kohvichus rass a eye meh huzbin mudda
wenn she ting dem a show

Faddahinla gett sweet, an muddahinla rock he
Lek a picknee dodo in she lapp
She deh havf he

Faddahinla a knock she
In abedeez lojee he deh lash she
Oh meh mamma

How faddahinla a beat she
He deh tek stick ann knock she bad

Alex Bacchus's other writings: 59, 91, 147

Simone Devi Jhingoor
Your Radha Needs You

You, my beloved have left me alone
in this world, I ache for you, yearn for you.
My body is now a barren wasteland
missing your tender touch that gave me life.
A chasm lies in my heart, the rupture
grows wider every passing day as I
try to recall the details of your face.
It's become as blurry as my eyesight
in my old age. Once intertwined with mine,
your soul has chosen to mesh with spirit.
I envy your shared bond with the divine.
Dream of when we can reunite, my love—
twin flames reconnecting as two magnets.
See you soon my Krishna, so we can dance.

Simone Devi Jhingoor's other writings: 65, 84, 133

Andre Bagoo
Chapter Two

That morning the radio was playing a song that felt familiar even if I didn't know the words, didn't understand the language. I recognized the grainy static, the tinny voice, the muffled beats as though they were my thrumming heart, as though they were the rain that had fallen last night on the galvanize roof as you slept on top of me smelling of too much cologne, your two Venezuelan friends huddled on a bed in the corner, and something rising in their chests like bread dough, breaths soft clouds now floating into the air as I dream out of the house, the yard, I pass the chickens, I pass the dogs and someone follows me—am I remembering correctly?—I have a strange feeling, as I did the night before, a feeling that there are sagas inside me waiting to be written, epics as heavy as the gold chain you wore as you thrust into me and I tried to muffle my moans because it was all so sketchy and even as I surrendered to pleasure I still thought the weight of your pendant slapping my flesh was like the weight of something I might one day carry, some foundation stone, some temple. I didn't know where the taxi stand was and I asked a man who gave me directions then decided he would walk the short distance with me. Later, I roamed Port of Spain knowing everybody could tell what I'd done, could smell the smoke from the club on me, could look into my eyes and see the drag queen, the pole dancer, the small room with walls of mirrors, the graveled yard outside on which footsteps crunch like whispered secrets and groups of friends look at each other cautiously, from a distance, because tomorrow is the question.

Andre Bagoo's other writings: 57, 112, 130

Eddie Bruce-Jones
Sansur

Dear God –

We will not go back
to die there,
in Sansur's home—
to be ruined
in the ice.

He drinks and drinks
a sweet aged brew
and leaves the shards sticky.
At night she times
the hard taps
and stores away their music.

Every day she shows off
all my things, all my things
to him.
I am to be consumed.
His eyes are greedy marbles.

She offers him
her lap,
now full of jewels,
a thousand shiny teeth.
Both mine and hers
he takes.

One beam from the hearth,
Father,
propping up the tiny hut—
he breaks
just like the music.

It lands,
like silence.

Eddie Bruce-Jones's other writings: 60, 99, 122

Anu Lakhan
Coming home

I fear the drunken,
wanton home of my husband.
His parents,
shameless and vile unto me,
keep a very small house.
And always, a stick is involved.

Did I mention the meanness of the house?

Anu Lakhan's other writings: 73, 110, 131

Will Depoo
Meh na gan sas and sasur

Meh nah gan sasur
He ah drink daru
Ah beat sas
Mek she pujay am
Sas ah watch meh
Meh cyan go latrin in peace
Meh na go

Will Depoo's other writings: 71, 87, 154

Natasha Ramoutar
No Joy Be

hum / no joy be / here to / greet / me / haha
no friends are / here / no / yaar here / baba

roads / roads / lead to / bottle's / bottom / he
speeds / to / dry / bottle's / lake, now / sasur / he

shares / his / greed / with / my mother / in law, way
above / me, she / wields stick / jabs, digs, pokes

not / jewelry / though she treats / him / baba
as gold / silver / tucked in her lap / how / baba?

when he / beats her / so sorry I am / here / baba
my needs / are more / than what's pared from / me / baba

when he / beats her / so sorry I am / here / baba
lake I / see the / lake now dry, hide / me / baba

Natasha Ramoutar's other writings: 72, 98, 120

Nicholas Peters

"Meh nah ah go dem in-law house, Daddy"

Meh nah ah go dem in-law house, Daddy.
Meh life gon turn miserable deh.

Day-in, day-out de man ah drink rum,
Day-in, day-out de lady ah annoy meh spirit.

Day-in, day-out de lady ah look through meh thing,
And all meh ah see is dey greedy life.

De man does tek swing at de lady, Daddy.
Then she does get anything she ah want.

He does steady beat de lady, Daddy.
In abbeh small small house,
De man got he own wood fuh she,
And he does beat duh big lady bad.

Daddy, meh nah want go dem in-law house.

Nicholas Peters's other writings: 63, 80, 124

Anita Baksh
Don't send me back, daddy

Na mek meh guh me fad-in-law house, daddy
Dem a control und watch me, daddy

Verse 1
Fad-in-law a drink rum everyday
Mud-in-law a gimme licks everyday

Verse 2
Mud-in-law a show all body me ting dem
Fad-in-law jealous a me

Verse 3
Mud-in-law and fad-in-law a swing together
He lie down pun she lap, daddy

Verse 4
Fad-in-law pounds mud-in-law
In abi small hut with no wall
He pound she with he hard wood

Anita Baksh's other writings: 55, 83, 136

Miranda Rachel Deebrah
Na Mek Me Go

Oh Fadda God

Na mek me go a me in-law dem house,
Life guh done if me go.
Na mek me go a me in-law dem house;
Please, please Fadda, na mek me go.

Whole day fadda-in-law a drink he rum,
Whole day mudda-in-law a beat me like drum.
Whole day
Whole day dem na done.

Life tek too much from me
an' ee na gi none.
Oh Fadda, if me go back a dem house
me whole life guh done.

Oh Fadda God, tek pity pon me;
How much ting in da house me see.
Mudda-in-law mek one swipe a she man
and he tun round an' beat she.

Mudda-in-law a beg for she life
but oh Fadda, no help na come.
Na! Me na go back deh, Fadda God;
If dem mek me, me guh run.

Miranda Rachel Deebrah's other writings: 64, 89, 152

Elizabeth Jaikaran
I Will Not Go to My Father-in-Law's Home

I will not go to my father-in-law's home, daddy.
I would re live the same day each day, daddy:

Verse 1
My new dad, in a perpetual drunken stupor.
My new mom, only benching me with cane.

Verse 2
My new mom, never satisfied with me.
My new dad, hungry for my gaze.

Verse 3
My mother-in-law's punches will be my new life, daddy.
I thought I was your sweet daughter, daddy.

Verse 4
My father-in-law will beat my mother-in-law, too, daddy.
The small home will be filled with her screams, daddy.
My father-in-law will beat my mother-in-law, too, daddy.
Each night I will see his stick on her back, daddy.

Elizabeth Jaikaran's other writings: 62, 82, 101, 140

Chandanie Somwaru
A next one was found in a barrel, body bloated

but watch
                how
allbody
                does tek dey eye
and pass that house
                where   the tulsi
is rotting
        jiyara
                is a cashew pear
fallen to the dirt
                        waiting for ants
to mouth the remains
                our bodies are stuffed
with sindoor
                the sky is thrown
into the dahl pot
                roosters
peck the feet
of jumbie following
behind sasur
tonguing bush rum
                from his chin
firewood is being rubbed
                between mudda in law's hands
fi jook meh
                fuh see
how to make sugar cake

                      from what leaks
watch dey so
                    as she
uses her fingers to catch
the last embers from the firewood
peels jiyara from her palms
                          buries
it with the fallen
tulsi
nobody waan da
            black black
dutty skin gyal
fuh mine
                    if she
suskay an' prayin'
                          meh nah waan dis oh lawd fadda
if she cyan
          tek mash
          wine she waist over her remains
dekhe nah,
                          how sasur does ketch
bad mind
a goat's head on his shoulders
leyley fallin' from he mouth
                      lookin fuh ram she
fuh claim the tika he
patkay on her forehead
                      with the soot
of firewood
                      see she back bend bend bend
              collecting
sindoor
          falling from her hair
crowding she patacake
all dem bloodclaat

                              swirling in the wash bin
as she sinks into
red lavender and lime
                    emerges
as chaaya
closing her eyes
                    she's by the jamuna
her lap decked with marigolds
to jhula jhule
                    sasur like nandalala
sticking her fingers in his mouth
the cream of her jiyara
lulling
            him

to sleep
            to sleep now
so tomorrow
the firewood will
collect again
          she'll come show meh
how fuh bun
                again
mudda in law will
bradang
                against
                              the wall
again
that house will start leaning over over over
bending like sas's back
                          how no one see sasur
come back with
firewood
even dem who does gyaff steady steady
            make no sound

around that house
turning away

meh foot ah bleed bleed
the screams

pierce my jiyara
the fence bruk down
but still no one watches
how meh cyan stan no more
no more

that house—

please father—

don't make me go back

Chandanie Somwaru's other writings: 66, 105, 128

FASTEN YOUR VEIL:

TRANSLATIONS

(Yusuff Khan 1980)

ĀJ	**SAWALIYĀ**	**SASUR**	**GHAR**	**JĀNĀ**
today	beloved	father-in-law	house	must go

Verse 1

CHUNARĪ	**PHENKE**	**PIYĀ**	**SE**	**MILENGĪ**	**SAĪYĀ**
veil	having worn	beloved	(to/from)	will meet	lover

TUM	**HO**	**CHATUR**	**SAIYANĀ**	**SASUR**	**GHAR**	**JĀNĀ**
you	be	intelligent	cunning	father-in-law	home	must go

ĀJ	**SAWALIYĀ**	**SASUR**	**GHAR**	**JĀNĀ**
today	beloved	father-in-law	house	must go

Verse 2

JO	**AB**	**DAAG**	**LAGI**	**CHUNARĪ**	**MEIN**
that	now	stain	marked	veil	in

TUMKO	**MARIKE**	**TAANA**	**SASUR**	**GHAR**	**JĀNĀ**
to you	having thrown	jeer	father-in-law	home	must go

ĀJ	**SAWALIYĀ**	**SASUR**	**GHAR**	**JĀNĀ**
today	beloved	father-in-law	house	must go

Verse 3

KEHET	**KABĪR**	**NIRGUN**	**PAD**	**HAI**
saying	Kabir	type of spiritual song	verse	is

SAMAJH SAMAJH	**RAHE JĀNĀ**	**SASUR**	**GHAR**	**JĀNĀ**
understand-understand	will be left	father-in-law	home	must go

ĀJ	**SAWALIYĀ**	**SASUR**	**GHAR**	**JĀNĀ**
today	beloved	father-in-law	house	must go

Divya Persaud
take your veil

you have worn your veil,
beloved,

now go meet him
at the house;

take that coveted
mind of yours—

father-in-law's house
awaits you.

your stained veil gathers
jeers; today,

you must go,
you must go;

as Kabir's verses
remain veiled,

beloved,
beloved,
go.

Anita Baksh
today beloved father-in-law house must go

Verse 1

Wear this orhni, beloved, and go meet your betrothed
Use your wits to outsmart them, you must go to your father-in law's home,
Today beloved, to father-in-law's house, you must go

Verse 2

Your veil has already been stained
You don't want bad name, you must go to father-in-law's home
Today beloved, to father-in-law's house, you must go

Verse 3

Like a verse from Kabir's song
So much is left unsaid, not understood, to father-in-law's home you must go
Today beloved, to father-in-law's house, you must go

Aliyah Khan
Chunari, Chunari

Aaj sawaliyaa
Sasur ghar jaanaa
Sasur ghar jaanaa.

Ey gyal
Galang a yuh fadda in law house
Put on yuh chunari and
galang and meet yuh saiyaa

(Gyal pickney tink she bright
But she going have to galang she way)

Put on yuh chunari and cover yuh head
Why de chunari dutty suh
Hide de stain beti
Or yuh guh pay

Galang a yuh fadda in law house
Chalo, chalo!

Gyal wha you know 'bout Kabir and nirgun?
Yuh wan' dead?
Samjhe?

Galang a yuh fadda in law house
Galang, gyal

Andre Bagoo
Big Daddy

Big Daddy wants me
wants life to go
back to when rivers flowed
everything stops
a cat pauses before prey
veil torn, he wants me

he wants to drink me
beat me out until I am drunk
on the shadows of a dream
my skin is now baize

Big Daddy's balls
Big Daddy's hut
and the codeword is sugar

Saints, I steal shoes
into tomorrow
this island shall be feet
slaughtered with a quill

Big Daddy
Big Daddy
big as a whale
freak Atlantic storm

with your acid pen
eye me a tiger
draw me a tongue
spit out, flag out
elseward a miracle

Saints, the world is mad

Alex Bacchus
Ayo Kyahnt Outrun Faddahinla Houws

Put on ayo orhni, gyal, time fi mek yuself proppah
Time kum fi see ayo maan, nah

How ayo klevvah nah mattah
Ayo faddahinla houws, now ayo muss go

Tiday, to faddahinla houws ayo go, gyal

Nomattah how ayo orhni stainup
Ann nomattah allbahdy guh laff yuh

Pick yuhself up
Time fi leff, to ayo faddahinla houws ayo go

Tiday to faddahinla houws abbe muss go

Kabir bina say in ee bhajan song
Ayo undahstaan?
To faddahinla houws ayo muss go

Time fi leff, ayo faddahinla houws ayo go

Eddie Bruce-Jones
Promises

I've been pious
waited so long
I will go home
to meet my love
today
with my head covered

You be smart,
cunning
my beloved
for now
I must go

But if
you make a mockery
stain your veil
then you will too
will be cast away—
understand

Having sung this verse
of the Nirgun song
hear me well
daughter
all that is left is the depth
of our promises

I am off to be with Sansur
today, now
beloved
I am going home

Kaneesha Cherelle Parsard
It is Your Time

Veil yourself, be ready for the journey
Neither wiles nor wit will save you
It is your time

Beti, it is too late to wash out the stain
They will laugh, yes, but
It is your time

Though you don't know the laments are for you
You know the way
It is your time

Elizabeth Jaikaran

Today, My Love, You Must Meet Our Greatest Love

Verse 1

Wrapped in your veil, my love, to meet our greatest love.

You will become enlightened, when you meet our greatest love.

Today, my love, you must meet our greatest love.

Verse 2

That veil around you is now stained,

That is the signal that you are being called home to our greatest love.

Today, my love, you must meet our greatest love.

Verse 3

I remember Kabir's spiritual songs

To help me understand where you are going: you have left to meet our
        greatest love.

Today, my love, you must meet our greatest love.

Nicholas Peters
"Baba, is time fuh go yuh In-Law House"

Baba, is time fuh go yuh In-Law House.

Nevermind how bright you bright,
Yuh Man ah wait for you, my dear.
All yuh thing dem get dutty heh,
And overso dem gon care for you.

Is just how Things are, Baba,
You gah fuh understan' duh.
By dem, yuh love gon care
For you, and start ayuh own house.

Is time fuh go your In-Law House, Baba.
Is time.

Miranda Rachel Deebrah
Return to God

Fasten your veil to become
Death's bride,
        Today you return to God.

Though you be bright,
sharp of wit and mind,
        Today you return to God.

Your veil is stained, marked with shame,
and all will laugh and jeer your name.
But listen well,
for this truth remains:
Beloved,
        You shall return to God.

Your homegoing draws near.
Sacred writings of Kabir —
Understand, understand
his lamentations, do you hear?
Beloved,
        You shall return to God.

You shall return to God.

Simone Devi Jhingoor
Separation

Beta, the day dem Arkati steal me from you,
me feel me lungs rip out me ribcage.
Air flow halt to me brain, I start fuh choke
from me shallow breath; de shock of grief
when me body sever from yuh one.
Long wata nah stop drop from me eye.

I tell yuh, love is we lifeline.

Mataji, me been ah wonda where yuh gone
Yuh disappear like how de clouds does hide de sun.
Everyday me ah look out fuh yuh,
to see if yuh face goh light up de horizon.
One deep hole deh inside me gut, it can't mend.
Me pain hollow like one old, dry coconut
that has fallen off de tree, no good to anyone.
Abee bond amputated by distance.

I tell yuh, love is we lifeline.

Here in Guyana me deh, from dawn until dusk
me ah wuk pon de field ah weed de ground
fuh mek sure nice suga cane can grow.
Sweeten dem tea, fatten dem British belly.
Abee deh two oceans apart, when we go see mati again?
Beta, mek sure yuh rememba yuh get one muddah.

I tell yuh, love is we lifeline.

Chandanie Somwaru
I'm tired of the men telling us

      Bring your shawl
come.
You see
    what it says here:

        Mata wore a dupatta when she split open
              bhumi—
    the jhumka
        whispering
           piya se milengi—
    the last view of her shaligram eyed

      love
  slipped
        between her
    skirts
as the doors closed
          behind
    her.

You have to
    You have to

    ghar jaana

you twist up your mouth
in the dupatta mother
skipped over fallen
okra on Liberty Ave for—
finding rhinestones that would place
a hundred suryas
on the crown of your head,
                    But

                                                    r
                                                    e
                                                    m
                                                    e
                                                    m
                                                    b
                                                    e
                                                    r

                    you're just clay
                                        molded
                            into pot
            into hands   that carry
            the pot
                        into sharp
            broken
                                earth
                                            after
            a missed step.

See
even then
            how clumps
of mothers lined
their mouths with camphor
    passed their children

the agarbatti
because they knew... they knew.

You have to
          You have to

                    ghar jaana

we've packed your arms
with pindas
here's your raft of kush grass

            don't
                look back

let the waves make you   the waves

              lost

makeyoulostletthewavesmakeyoulostmakeyoumakeyou

make you—

                    Knock. *Piya se
milenge.*

Krystal M. Ramroop
Today, the Dulahin Leaves for Sasur's Home

Verse 1

Beloved, you will adorn yourself with a veil to meet your lover.
Despite your wit and stubbornness, you must go to your father-in-law's home.
Today, beloved, you must go to your father-in-law's home.

Verse 2

Now that your tears stain your veil
and though taunts are thrown at you, you must still go to your father-in-law's
        home.
Today, beloved, you must go to your father-in-law's home.

Verse 3

Kabir's bhajan reveals that God will protect you, beloved.
Understand this: nothing is left here for you; you'll have to leave your
        childhood home.
Today, beloved, you must go to your father-in-law's home.

Nadia Misir

today, beloved, you must leave for yuh sasural house

ornhi over your hair,
you left to meet your lover.
yuh propa bright, but,
beloved, today you must
leave for his home. yuh orhni
stain up and dem go
put dem mouth pon yuh—
today you must leave for
your beloved's home.
wha yuh know about
Kabir, about he sorrow?
aj sawaliya sasur ghar jana.

Will Depoo
Fadda-in-law house

Beta, yuh mus go ah yuh fadda-in-law
Yuh geh sense
Yuh veil stain
Wah dem gon seh?
Yuh mus undastand
If yuh nah wan suffa
Yuh mus go

Natasha Ramoutar
Today, Be Loved

today / you must go now / be loved / go / must go

veil, now we / can see / the ties / that / bind soul to / soul here
leave / your / wise thoughts / tucked at home / be loved / go / must go

today / you must go now / be loved / go / must go

the / stain / that / cradles / fabric like / mine
only / draws forth jeers / leave now / be loved / go / must go

today / you must go now / be loved / go / must go

what now / of wise / verse you / left / leave
Kabir's / dirges / at home / must go / be loved / go / must go

today / you must go now / be loved / go / must go

Anu Lakhan

Yamraj, even prayer is hidden from me

my lover is a disguise
my jest is a disguise
my scarred sandwriting is a disguise

but death has seen me

still

ॐ सूर्यपुत्राय विद्‌महे महाकालय धीमहि तन्नो यम: प्रचोदयात

O Yamraj, even prayer is hidden from me

FRACTALS I:

THE AFTERLIVES OF CHUTNEY

Suzanne C. Persard

At a karaoke bar on 101ˢᵗ Avenue in Richmond Hill

A body drinks too much rum, balances the glass on his head
crying, "Hum na jaibe, kabui ghur mein baba"
believes this canto of rum was the first voice
he heard of his own father, whom he only knew
through songs of that place they called home.
"Hum na jaibe," he croons under a disco of fire lights
his echoes transport him from this old haunt.
A man clinks car keys against Heineken bottles,
makeshift dhantal transporting him in time.
A darkened rum bar in Queens is no cane field
nor estate, nor plantation. A rum bar in Queens
is another place for home. As he sings words he knows
by heart, he would never know a hundred years past,
his great-grandmother hummed a similar tune,
unglamourous & uncited, her voice out of joint in time.

Suzanne C. Persard's other writings: 100, 118

Nadia Misir
Chutney Poem

my mother tells me these songs
bless the dance floors
of bottomhouse weddings back home,
of backyard matikoor nights
and living room sport-ups
in richmond hill.
bless the bar girls
tending bar not far from
the shadow of the A train & J train.
bless the storefronts bearing names like
Hibiscus, Nest, New Thriving, Kaieteur.
liquor bottles line up against the wall like cane,
the gutter floods with rain wata
and i remember my grandfather
recounting how to flood a field
before planting rice while we watched cars
zoom down 109 avenue.
i did not know plantation,
but plantation found me
in the el dorado bottles living in wall units,
in the chutney lyrics leaking out of bars
on karaoke nights on to the streets outside,
in the wailing voices of those
we call high up.
bless the waist that rotates
and rolls to the beat
despite the beatings
happening all around,
bless the fingers that fly

across the harmonium's mourning keys
bless the wrists that knock di tassa.
praise the bottomhouse dance floor,
the backyard wedding. praise those
who dance with abandon. praise the pot spoon
that flies up into the air when the dholak sounds.
praise the boombox and the cassette tapes
stacked up like scripture.

Aliyah Khan
"Guyana kay dulahin migrate to America"

Guyana kay dulahin migrate to America
Subhaji gyal come off de plane in one miniskirt

She done wid de matapee, she wukkin at Kennedy,
She wearing chunari and ohrni pon Liberty

She calling it dupatta, she calling it hijab
She praying in mandir and masjid calling pon she *rabb*

She minding backra pickney
She mekking she U.S. money

Nana still drinking white rum
and Nani drinking wine

One New Year's Day on 103
Nana make ah mistake

and cut Nani throat

Nicholas Peters
On this threshold

On this threshold,
Tenacious tassas
Beckon her to transform.

In a rumshop stall,
They wait amid
The piss and vomit.
Her hands in Her hands,
Leaving drunken shouts,
For the solace of
Her breath.

By the door she pauses,
Tumeric adorned,
Hibiscus trailing.
Percussions pull
His bride and joy
Into a lesson of
Waist trembling, and lovemaking.

At In-Laws' gate,
Among the masala twilight
And blasting stereo,
She hesitates.
The trench a comma
Between her lives:

His loyalty, Her passion –
My choice,
Tassa beats in tow.

On each threshold
Transformed—
Dulahin to Aji.
Yet, across this bridge
Reborn.

Elizabeth Jaikaran
In Good Humor

Pa's freedom is new violence.
Ma's freedom is a new cage.
My freedom
       is in recognizing
that there is none.
There is nothing in this place
for me.
My freedom
       is in laughing
at the idea of freedom.
In all of my lives, that has
never been mine.
               You knew all of this.
               And you sent me anyway.

Anita Baksh
Marriage

From birth she prepared for it,
her goal unconscious.
find a good boy from a good family
love can't buy ting from store

The shimmering ohrni on her head,
keeps de bad eye away.
De bride change tree times,
like film star: yellow, red, then blue lengha

The groom arrives draped in silk juragama,
a canary poised on his mur.
Watch how he nice and fair-skin,
and he guh college too.

Under matriarch's new house rules,
layers of silence cloak her truth.
Dis nah you house.
Yuh family dem can't come hay.

Baby-child bites at her nipples.
The slit between her thighs burns.
What a nice bai pickney she make.
De baby look jus like he daddy.

Ohrni: veil
Lengha: an Indian outfit (top, skirt and veil/shawl)

Juragama: long robe worn by groom
Mur: head piece worn by groom

Simone Devi Jhingoor
Childhood Days Gone

I was green as an unripe mango.
Girlish in my thoughts and shape—
A board for a chest, no coke bottle waist.
Still dreaming of dancing like Helen.

Married off to an older man visiting
from a place in 'Merica called Rich Man Hill.
My life stagnated like un-sprouted seeds.
No longer did it solely belong to me.

Then again, did my life ever belong to me?
To them, I was a rental car never driven,
handed from my parents to a stranger.
I wept before getting on the plane.

He often left me alone to fend off his family.
I dreaded my father-in-law's leathery, prune face
tracing my every move with glazed eyes,
desire dripping down his rum soaked mouth.

His wife endured his drunken wrath
while I hid in the other room, anxious
for his stormy mood to pass. So did his son,
arriving home minutes after the false calm set in.

I longed for my not so long ago childhood days.
Remembering the way my legs used to sink
knee deep into muddy backdam roads
not a worry in the world; dunkedam.

I prayed for that kind of carefree joy again.

Krystal M. Ramroop
Bidaai

Oh, beautiful one
bejeweled in your
ancestors' gold, your
supple skin glows like
the sacred fire.

Oh, beautiful one
garbed in the finest
silk, sindoor, kajal-
stained, safeguarded by
your veil from nazar.

Oh, beautiful one
with gentle strides, youth
dissipates. Your heart
trembles in sync to
the dholak, dhantal.

Oh, beautiful one
your lover's name etched
in your mehndi,
a new beginning,
a new family.

Oh, beautiful one
stubborn, graceful, brave,
this is your life now:
sasural, pati,
beta, beti, tum.

Oh, beautiful one
will you seek refuge
under the neem tree
with your open wounds,
with emerging scars?

Oh, beautiful one
as your hand slips mine,
a feeling of dread,
heartache engulfs me
as you bid farewell.

Will Depoo
Nah tek yuh eye and pass meh

She mus respect she in-laws
Expect fuh dem wuk she like a horse
Geh on she knees fuh dab deh bottom house
Why does she need to do this?
Isn't marriage a union?
Dem mus respect you
She nah haffi poojay dem
Yuh nah haffi deal wid sufferation
Daru nah excuse fuh abuse
Nah leh dem tek yuh eyes and pass yuh
Leh abi brek tradition

Divya Persaud
pardes

she stood at the seaside—
payal threaded stone—
their song made them chide her—
that day she left her home—

> *does the tide show your face?*
> *foam veils your eyes.*

and in her heart she clenched—
that taste of blood of man—
that intellect unwrenched—
her feet adorned of sand—

> *do murti return your gaze—*
> *his kurta's stench?*

her mouth swallowed the day
as salts churned—wasted
against the throngs—the fray—
her hungry mouth—betrayal—

> *you enemy of man*
> *you enemy of man*

Miranda Rachel Deebrah
For My Sister

Sister,
I see you,
I hear your plea
for a life free from pain,
free from hurt and shame.
Life not guaranteed to
we who born
girl child
who guh grow and become
    Woman.

Sister,
I shed tears
for both you and me
knowing that
no matter what we do,
Death
is always a possible outcome,
never off the table —
A tragic circumstance of being
    Woman.

Sister,
I wonder
how many before us
have met
Death in disguise
and dined
and danced with him

before he took them away?
Their only crime being
 Woman.

Sister,
Your cries long since passed
echo forward into the present.
I hear you say,
"Me na go back" —
Well let me set your heart at ease:
Gyal, yuh nah gaffa go back,
there is another way
to live in your freedom as
 Woman.

Sister,
Me hear dem old time song
seh "You shall return to God".
And yes, indeed you shall,
but in your triumphant return
Liberation and Healing
awaits you and me,
awaits all those
honoured to be called
 Woman.

Sister,
In your name,
the marks on your veil are washed away
as a prayer falls from my lips
and a vow:
Through your daughters now
and in days to come,
you will know
the power you hold in being
 Woman.

Alex Bacchus
Kissmehass Rum Sukkah

Beer, rum and whiskey,
they smell of it all and chant

        rum   is   life

a mantra
no proper pandit's words
could ever come to hold meaning

all the lands of sugar plantations
know this story too well

    di rumdrinka
                nonm-la ki ka bwé wonm
                                  el borracho e o
                             bêbado

Their grandfathers
our grandfathers
yours and mine
and theirs and theirs

bound and not bound
chained and not chained

cut the cane and boiled
it down fi drink

the sickness started long, long ago

before yu born
befor meh bina tek brett

Every El Dorado bottle
a karry jumbie
pon ee sail ann mast

Yu guh be real maan demma say
just like the British tought uu
and brainwashed us
with all their rules to our dismay

Dem wann fi nno yu real maan lek dem
whach di redd kriket ball nokk ee wicket
ann a Banks inna haan
demma hoo a suhk rum alldeylaang

4 o'clock in the afternoon
and 4 o'clock in the morning
the soca ann chutney chune a play

Bottle caps line the ground,
an invasive species taking over
like the ones that ripped out the mangroves

Red-starred Heineken and golden-crowned Budweiser disks,
the caps maimed and bent,
popped off, one after another
buss up lek dem woman ann piknee
the ones dem shut and shove
like the clapped roti they devour from their wives' hands
without an ounce of gratitude

ravenous dogs

But those caps scatter across the ground

with each of the awkward pounds and jerks
and every one of their unrhythmic seismic stomps

DOOM,
             BOOM,
                         BOOM

Di drunk maan tigeda,

trying?

what a sad, sad attempt

to whine up dem waist
but you know how drunk karibbyan maan a be

Many harams to count,
so many harams to make sense of

But maan ann neks maan a dans,

They dance together
what your heart deep down wanted

desire they made you fear,
desire they shame and hate

just like you hate all the childhood nightmares
filled with their booming, boozy laughs,
waking you up in sweat, tears, and panic in the middle of the night

A real man's drink
you'll never have

a maan
yu nah havf fi be

ann
real maan
dem nevvah guh be

You, ayo
we, abedeez
the theydies, the girls, and the gays
ann na figett di transmook babes
lime ann sip pon yuh wine
ann lil lil bit ov rum
in the colourful sparkly drinks
shittalkin
all those duttystinken men

whine up yuh wicked waiss
with the magic of your chamkay
                                soca
dancehall,
            ann chutney
      chune
                        a play
jukk it up

      with

                and to make joy

Waystmaan nevvah di way
ann pay no attenshun a wha demma say,
aunty ann uncle taat namattah

no maan konchrol yuh, gyal
no maan, no wumaan, no puhrson
only ayo kyan do it, gyal

your divine beauty and absolute freedom
they'll never know
they'll never have or own,
and never forget you're not alone!

Your men, your brothers,
your lovers and their mothers
better treat you right
and anyone with a second thought or who gets in the way
needs to get the fuck out of sight

FRACTALS II:
AND SOMETIMES VOICES WAKE

Natasha Ramoutar
Modulation

today / you must go now / beloved / go / must go

hum / the sound / that stories make / echo and
pulse / held / in dholak's beat / bounce / flounce / simmer

today / you must go now / beloved / go / must go

untrained ears / can mix words / and trained / more so
alchemic / exchange / we fade bruises here

today / you must go now / beloved / go / must go

we flesh / new noses / from clay / shed burned skin
like holy snakes / morph beloved / to be loved

today / you must go now / beloved / go / must go

bring bottles / back to sea / scrawl our stories /
yes I have / adjusted / the ropes / and yes

today / you must go now / beloved / go / must go

the dholak / sings in tune / with me / (with *hum*)

Eddie Bruce-Jones
Soon come

She died at noon. The phones were birds. Deep wooden bowls began to fill with coconut, grated, ready to be squeezed. Tables were laid with too much food. Goat, tripe, rum, meat patties someone bought in a rush, fish fry, plantain, black cake, and roti—mountains on all the counter tops. One long year she laid in the bed. Tears gathered into a pepper pot. All the fingers of dumpling and palms of meat. The tapping of serving spoons and the occasional cry of a flute. No words were made possible. Only the warm envelope of the kitchen could hold time. A reunion of the happiest remainders, as sordid as the present tense, as fragile and thin as the windchimes. The smiling lips, it was agreed, would part just to taste, to devour, and with that life, to mourn only when the food was done. Soon come.

Suzanne C. Persard
In a corner of Hindu Town

A voice sounds. A sarangi player
fiddles to the tune of night, a mouth
accustomed to swallowing pain
unclenches jaw. A throat swells, bellows
Hum na jaibe, mi nah guh guh
to that place of rum-soaked poison
hum na jaibe, mi nah guh guh
to that prison of flesh, this island.

Mi nah guh guh, mih ah guh get lick
in that drunken Gehenna of daubed roof & straw
in that estate of May Pen, of Monymusk
of Hanover. I wander the night sick,
Hum na jaibe, sasur ghar mein baba
to that river of Styx, drowned by cane
I will not go, I will not go, father
Hum na jaibe, sasur ghar mein baba
to that place whose name is *home.*

Elizabeth Jaikaran
The bereaved explains her route to jannah, or, how the churail lost her eyesight

Knock on the door.
I've learned that the beating blood in my ears
is the percussion of angels' footsteps.
I try to march with them. Single
file and shining.
But I am but a ragged churail in the procession
with embers for feet, and ash for tongue.
 Peep in.
I behold vinegar in streams.
Singing my cheeks, cleaning me
like raw chicken meat in a metal basin.
The smell never gone just yet.
 Turn the key.
There is no escape from madness
but to fall directly into her arms.
An inky road of currants unfolds
and I bend to save from losing myself in
all of the dark.
 Wipe your feet.
I must make wu'du to see you now.
In a pattern of madness and worship
I see you in flashes of divinity.
But nowhere else.
 Walk in.
I turn to leave the road of currants.
Propelling one wretched foot after another.

In a procession of angels
leading to you,
    Tell Mama Chin Chin, "morning!"
And at the end of the marching
I prostrate with a million angels
at the sight of beauty that feels like an embrace,
and spend the rest of my life
trying to undo my eyes.

Kaneesha Cherelle Parsard
The Coolie Woman Climbs Out of the Portrait

She follows the path her eyes cut

beyond the right fr—
beyond the barracks, her husband's grasp. Past the arrivants gathered
for their first photograph: some squatting, others standing, all unused
to space after the long journey. Back to her jahaji-mati, before they
scattered to the estates. Or to the plots, seeding watering tilling
alongside women and men like and unlike her. Or to her yet-unborn
great-grand, like and unlike her, who can't see but feels her near.

The great-grand stares at an image, imagining the coolie woman
climbing out and

Divya Persaud
jewel

wind entrain a

                mote

                        turn it cumulus

    in sky house

                        grow sharp

I

                diamond

                                  rise

earth hot house

                            grow teeth

    melt

Chandanie Somwaru
To the women who've left their bodies

I've started

hanging

my camel

skin on tree branches

how

I [   ]

in moonlight

how my   flaccid

fingers

c

r

o

o

k

[   ]

call me

back

into [   ]

[   ] the story

⌈   ⌉

‒

Did you hear? Shanti lined her door with rice last night, but she still felt a tongue slithering around her wrist. She opened her eyes, shoved away the skinned body sucking on her breasts, tried to call out *hey ram*, but she was locked in her own reflection.

Or this? My nani told me a man could jump through a hundred windows but you can only jump through one. And if you did, that means you must have done some obeah in the backyard or let
a cricket into the house or got caught trying to ride a dolphin with a trident in your hands.

Wait, I got that wrong. It was something about riding on snakes in the middle of the ocean and Annapurna giving us the rice grown from her arms but we're supposed to be grounded at a man's feet.
Who else can   protect   you from   yourself   when Kali's howl foams out of your mouth?

—

106

I'm turning rancid
       with words stuck
in between my teeth
it's been too long since I've
       fingered myself until
chameli leaks down my thighs
until I feel what it's like
to soak in blood that isn't mine
          my mother let her child
slip out of her
         drop by drop
because father said—
          I must
chup chup
          chew the words back up
      but
I walk down the street
        backwards chanting
I'm going to be dust anyway
            I'm going
to be   *dust*
           any way
    I'm go   *ing to be*
      d

         u
      s

        t

any
     way

—

Is this how it feels to be a girl   who climbed a tree in the middle of
      the night
                  I've gotten too much side eye
                        too much *dis gyal need jurrey*   rubbed
                        down with mustard oil   I spark
                                    into the havan kund
      crumble into samagri and ghee   reignite until my spine

arches like a peacock feather   here   comes
the cutlass
                        prem
his wife's half
                                          severed head
but tonight the village
                        decided to burn the trees
            the sucker plant I've watered
      with *dukhiyon ko dukh dur kare*
                                    tells me I can't hide here
I found Puwa coiled   in our keyhole
                  Nani is moulting
                              back into child
dakshina pandit has come   with ganga jal   with words
                  firerass
                                                douse
                  I know you: thunderstorms
                  unzipping
      night with electrified tears   you: bodiless
                        women   unchoking   on rivers
            swollen with   stillborn fish-   eyed
girls
have told me to run
                  but just this once   while
                  my chest is
                        unfastened   my legs are
                        unraveled   by crisped trees
                                    while

108

the burners

        are clutching for breath

                while I'm buffering
                into shape

    let me soak

            the story

let me
      chase   away

—

      [contort]

[eyes with illusions]

        [containment]

[easily]

      [begins]

Anu Lakhan
Off-Off Broadway String Ensemble

[Transcript]

I'm not going to that house, going to that house,
going to that house where I'll die.

Whether it's a house, coffin or a couch:
it's a box and you're locked inside. Stay

home, stay in bed, don't you get it in your head,
It's the love you're feeling for him. It's your

clock, it's your friends, don't you listen to them.
Stay clear of eligible men. Don't be

going to that house, going to that house, going to that
house 'coz you'll die. I'm not going to that house, going to that house,

going to that house, where I'll die!

Off-Off Broadway String Ensemble

Andre Bagoo
Hurricane Erasures

> The sky, it seems, would pour down stinking pitch
> — Shakespeare, *The Tempest*

CATEGORY 3

           my son

Our revels now are

    melted into
             fabric

        the   globe itself
          shall dissolve

Leave   We
    are

       weakn   troubled:
     disturb'd   infirm

        turn   walk,

CATEGORY I

             father lies;
his

                   eyes:
            fade
       sea-change

           ring his knell

the isle is full of
hurt
a thousand twangling instruments
hum   and sometime voices
wake

clouds   open and show riches
drop   on me   wake
dream

He

made up his mind to leave

he could

disappear

in

the wind

Cane had been the destiny of his father,
indentured
in the burning sun.
he thought:

London, perhaps,

Canada

He   was

a carpet of soft petals.

ON CHUTNEY

Suzanne C. Persard

From Kingston to the Bronx: Chutney as Transporting

In the 1990s, in backyards over jerk smoke in New York City, playing a chutney cassette signaled a turn of the evening: that return to the beginning. Makeshift dhantaals were borne from car keys and Heineken bottles, and inevitably a tabla would be produced from thin air. To me, this ability to recreate the atmosphere of a satsang in a living room floor in the Bronx or Tampa or Toronto has remained a gorgeous tradition of the indentured. The old folk songs of Jamaica were my favorites, and in particular, this one song titled, "Bansuriwale." As a kid, like many kids my age, I was not aware of the meaning of old Indo-Jamaican folk songs. But the affective nostalgia at the start of a chutney was transporting: a different temporality emerged. Chutney signaled a wind-down of the evening and for a moment, everyone in the room seemed to conjure up the spirits of an ancestral past that we were somehow a century removed from, but still somehow tethered to; this complication of home is what I attempted to convey in the poems above. "Home" contains multiple geographic locations for descendants of the indentured and their diasporas, and as is the case with the second poem, one recites lyrics without knowing the translation of such lyrics—because the lyrics conjure this affective relationship to home. I still feel haunted when I turn on chutney songs. Such feelings are untranslatable— even as the very genre has emerged and taken on new lives and sonics. Researching chutney music many years after childhood, I realized that so many of the songs were actually performed initially by women, as was it seems this popular Sundar Popo song. There is another level of haunting to this: women's voices somehow remain even when their voices are not in the most popular versions, as in the case of "Hum Na Jaibe." For me, the process of translation was negotiating the sound with how I imagined the Indians in Jamaica would have gathered around fires singing, as in one colonial report where a British officer stops in his tracks to listen to the Indians singing and celebrating at night. The colonial description is almost haunting, as the officer does not expect bodies to be out at night. I recall the white clothing that many Indians were photographed wearing during the period of indenture in Jamaica, as white is the color of Hindus during burial; the photographs were evocative of the paradox of something holy and violent. Chutney folk songs, for me, remain a kind of ancestral haunting.

Natasha Ramoutar

For me, chutney music was one of the first access points I had to my Indo-Guyanese heritage as someone born and raised in Toronto. I fondly remember the songs that would play in the car on long drives or at family congregations like birthday parties and weddings. As someone who has always loved storytelling, I naturally gravitated towards art forms like music and dance which had tales woven in the fabric of their being. However, I lacked access to the lyrics in chutney music because I did not speak Hindi. Instead of the stories I had been in search of, I found myself engulfed in aspects like cadence and tone. The upbeat nature of the music—both with the vocalists and with the musicians on the instrumental backing—created a more positive, celebratory image in my mind. This translation project and the ongoing reality of gender-based violence was a stark reminder that there is a dissonance between the tone of these songs and the reality of the story being told.

The process of coming to these translations and writing my response poem incorporated both my lack of understanding Hindi and the reality of gender-based violence. From a technical standpoint, I attempted to preserve the meter of the original song by mimicking the syllables of each word and using a slash to mark where the end of the word would be in its original form. While I chose to keep some of the Hindi words in their original form, I also attempt to translate certain sounds into English. This created imperfect creations such as pulling lake from lakrī and lakariyā or using road in place of roj. Both of these choices lead the translation to nonsensical line breaks and unintelligible meanings throughout the pieces. Thematically, I chose to incorporate the reality of gender-based violence by changing the tone of each translation. Instead of the celebratory atmosphere which is conveyed in the musical tracks, my translations are much more sombre and distressed. The response poem was an attempt to reclaim power from the point of view of the survivors in the translations.

The narrator(s), which shift throughout from a single narrator to a group of narrators, are able to retune both the lyrics and the dholak as a symbolic reclamation of power. This is also reflected in their reinvention of certain words that appeared in the previous translations, such as bottles and hum, and with their healing of injuries.

Eddie Bruce-Jones

The Urn

Mother brought him with her when she visited me in England, and she left him here. "Well, he's your grandfather, keep him for a while." Here he stayed, in an urn on my shelf, for nearly ten years. The gravitational pull the elders have, to draw the memories into any space and make them live, was the guidance I needed in my thirties to settle into a sense of self. A year ago, she called the urn back. Having dreamt so often of her father in recent times, she wanted him near. I should mention, the deal was always that we were going to spread his ashes over water, maybe the Ganges or the Rio Minho. But the reality was that the urn was a grounding force, a safety net for us—not for worship, but for a certain form of meditation. There was a magnetic weight, a temporally liminal presence, like the photograph of a *feeling* or the haptics of memory.

In chutney music, the energy of celebration is like an undercurrent that pulls along all imaginable life, but with the confident dissonance of the party that accompanies the funeral.

I realise, translating these poems, that chutney music is, for me, at the outer limits of my accessibility. I have to nestle up to Bhojpuri via English and standard Hindi and with the help of trusted resources. It feels like I am searching the tip of my tongue for the name of a childhood friend. The upbeat energy of the music is perfunctory, and I wrestle against my own sensibilities to listen for the shards of the pain and prayer, modest shadows floating on a lyrical verse, well-hidden in innumerable ripples of sparkly crystalline sweetwater. The pain of memory is surely sweeter than the emptiness of forgetting. This is what loss really means—the possibility of failure in the relentless fullness of chutney music. The layers upon layers of syncopation, self-referential and complete, give energy and demand energy in equal measure. The layers protect against the true pain of losing the story through some fissure in the sound—in the tentative communication across generations, places and tongues.

Translating these songs reminded me of the nature of violence and death, as both public and private. In one sense, the songs are intimate, addressed to family or the self or perhaps to a god or a lover. But they are also public incantations, playful storytelling, prayers for relief, ruminations on the social order of things. That is to say, these songs are meant to be legible to all those with the knowledge and experience to access them. One recognises the perfunctory nature of gender violence, the role of alcohol abuse in ordering the social lives of some of our elders and contemporaries, and the reverence for family and particularly parents and in-laws in the very conceptualisation of adult life, death and redemption.

In a way, death, violence and ideas of specific social orders are held, frozen in time, for scrutiny alongside the idea of a good life. The aspirational quality of the music—the dholak, the flute and the tassa—devours the pain, integrating it. Like a palimpsest, the light cheery music consumes some of the blade of the words, and indulges a deep longing for a world that comes into being just beyond reach. In this sense, 'going to Sansur's home' is both physical and unbounded, and 'home' is both a memory and a future, and its location is fixed and ephemeral. It is a place in the heart and mind, and it is right here, under our feet. Part of it dies when the song ends, but some part of it is always right where we are standing.

In announcing to the elders whether one will go home to be accountable to the moralistic expectations (or perhaps the memory) of a good life, we report home. The report may not be consistent with the demands or criteria of deliverance, and that may be a source of sadness; but there is a profound respect in establishing the truth of one's story that also demonstrates accountability to a life worth living. This report, then, is also a love letter to the innermost self, living in the urn on the shelf.

Nicholas Peters

Chutney music occupies a perennial space in my life because of how present it is in daily life in Guyana. It wasn't until I left Guyana for a prolonged period that I began to miss its seemingly ever-present rhythm in my life. This was true, not only for chutney but, for so many aspects of Guyanese life—like creolese, food, and music— that were part of me yet existed outside of me. This caused a lot of reflection from my part on the balance between the internal and external elements that shape who we are. For this writing process, I delved deeper into this reflection and what it meant for the choices we make, that ultimately determine how we exist in this reality. Through working on this project, I realised that chutney, despite being sung in Bhojpuri, communicates wholly Caribbean experiences which connect intimately to my Guyanese identity. Chutney continues the Caribbean custom of "talking back" to authority that we can find in many aspects of our culture, whether in literature, music, or daily life. Both songs when read together function as a discourse that captures the experiences Caribbean women have, as they touch on themes of filial piety, spiritual duty, personal autonomy, abuse, and death.

Underlying both songs is a sense of tension. This tension resonated with me as I contemplated my heritage and my ancestors' experiences of navigating their identity in a new land after leaving India. Chutney music captures this tension effectively because of its foundation in Indian culture and its incorporation of Afro-Caribbean elements. Personally, this tension is ever-present as someone who claims both my Afro and Indo heritages—two identities in Guyana that are projected as being in conflict with one another but by my existence and in the expression of chutney music prove that they can create beautiful things. I chose to translate both poems into creolese because encoded in this language is the shared history that these ethnic identities have in the same space.

Chutney music as a type of literature was also the catalyst for understanding my queerness as the genre allows men to experiment with their performative masculinity through dance. Some of my fondest memories of chutney come from the Hindu weddings of my family and friends, particularly on "Dig Dutty" or "Maticore" night. These nights would be my favourite because of the tassa drums' presence and their ability to release tension during a period that can be particularly stressful for women. Weddings and drums together possess profound transformative properties in certain Guyanese ceremonies. This in addition to the marital themes of both songs influenced how I wrote my poem. This process allowed me to contemplate aspects of my queerness and heritage; how these identities relate to each other; how familial duty and personal freedom clash, and how a woman could respond to, resolve, and escape these internal tensions. Good chutney finds a way to express these tensions in its musicality and performance, as it, too, continues to transform.

Aliyah Khan

"Ham Na Jaibe" and "Aaj Sawaliyaa" are the songs of my childhood in Guyana. I cannot read the lyrics; I only hear them sung in my head. I do not remember how old I was when I learned the songs. But what I realize now, in this translation and transposition, is that it's not Sundar Popo and Yusuff Khan, but Babla and Kanchan, singing to me from the recesses of my Guyanese memories.

Babla and Kanchan's versions of our Bhojpuri-Hindustani songs are more popular in the Indo-Caribbean. We may know our Sundar Popo, but who hear 'bout Yusuff Khan besides some old-time Trinis? We of the Indian diaspora love that B & K Bollywood playback sound. And I include all the descendants of that early coolie labor diaspora.

Where else I hear B & K besides at Caribbean parties and in Caribbean homes? At Bombay Curry Shop in Cape Town, South Africa in 2005. As I waited for my mince rooti—curry mince wrapped up in a roti just like in Trinidad—another piece of T & T piped through the plastic radio on the counter: Sundar Popo's "Kaisay Banie," as covered by B & K, over a countertop in Africa.

But how much Babla Shah and he wife Kanchan love us? They start coming with Mukesh and ting from the Indian film industry fuh check out de scene in Trinidad starting in 1967. When Indian ethnomusicologist Tejaswini Niranjana interview old Babla in 2003, he seh: "That music is very raw. Their singing is in their own style. They don't speak Hindi, and their accent is more Trinidadian accent . . . they [Indo-Trinidadians] have no grammar, and the words have no meaning sometimes." Well is still captivate they captivate enough to issue three-four album tiefing people song. Even Byron Lee and Arrow they cover; is "Kuch Garbar Hai" yuh know, or "Hot Hot Hot"? You can still buy Babla and Kanchan albums more easy than Sundar Popo whole original discography.

And what about Indians in Guyana? We never really had a Sundar Popo, and the Indo-Guyanese musical scene was never as well developed as in Trinidad. Chutney-soca is mostly Trini in its formation, and truth be told, is Babla and Kanchan really develop it too. The Surinamse, the lucky ones who still speak Hindoestani, do their propagation part I don't mean we cyah sing Hindi bhajan and Urdu qaseeda. But everybody in the Caribbean know that even though Guyana have more Indians, it was always more racially distress than anybody. Sugar estate and village more spread out than in South Trinidad. Continental country. El Dorado, Roraima, Kaieteur: the Amazon. But also Port Mourant, Crabwood Creek, Black Bush Polder: Indo-Guyana. Always a strange country, B.G.

"Ham Na Jaibe" and "Aaj Sawaliyaa" together are haunting and haunted songs about how Hindu and Muslim coolie gyal (like me; I am the fullaman variant) must go to she father-in-law house whether she wan' go or not. As in India, so in Guyana and Trinidad and Surinam.

I neither stayed home nor went to any father-in-law house. Leggo me na raja! as B & K by way of Halima Bissoon seh. Such a decision had other familial and personal consequences, which I sure is why my grandmother does haunt me. Is de twenty-first century an' ting now, nuff ah we in America and Canada and Inglan' an' ting, but Indian people doh change. How yuh/you/tum/aap keeping these days, eh? We deh.

"Aaj sawaliya" calls itself a nirgun bhajan like Kabir own. So maybe the song is that kind of worship metaphor: galang to your own divinity Marajin, Subhaji gyal. I think I doing that.

1. When I first started translating these songs word by word using my father's worn dictionary, why did it feel like I was being shoved underwater?

2. Salt from the ocean is unforgiving. Take it away from its home and it'll settle into your lungs, crystallize into a pebble. No voice or breath. Is this how the women in these songs drowned into the silence of Sundar Popo's melody, the clumping of the dholak beating faster and faster until the music became salt?

3. Why did I ever pelt waist to these songs?

4. When everybody gets too drunk at a house fete and the DJ yells into the mic, "we're going back to the big chunes," why do these songs play?

5. Have you ever felt that music was just too hard to catch . . . like a stagnant, white 8.5 x 11 inch paper couldn't possibly imitate the way the musician flicked his wrist against the dholak to make that high *tan* sound?

6. How much can a person speak when salt is lining their throat?

7. When I came face to face with the women in these songs, why did they swat at my fingers, etch their words into my palms until I started writing farther and farther from the lyrics and closer to the stories of women like them, women who end up like them, women who are them?

8. Was I reading too much into it?

9. Can the slowing down of words, the spaces between them or the lack of space between them be an indicator of tempo in music?

10. Did you get that the change of font size was the change of pitch in the word "jaana"?

11. Or no?

12. Are women only allowed to get married, die, and become jumbies who have to be killed again?

13. Is one death not enough?

14. Is it too late to say I'm sorry to the mothers who've lost their lives due their husbands' need to feel like they had some sort of power?

15. My aunt, having more than two glasses of red wine on a Friday night, told me to get married and then proceeded to tell me about the man back home who used to beat his dark-skinned wife. I thought why didn't anyone help her?

16. Why should I silence the women in these songs even more?

17. Am I a bad translator for allowing the woman who is begging her father not to go back to her father-in-law's house to speak more?

18. In my head, when I heard *ghar jaana*, I kept thinking about the funeral rituals for this woman; how easily they were ready to let this woman go, like dropping her ashes in the ocean was dropping an empty plastic bottle in the trash can, you know?

19. I still feel their words in my palms, asking me to hold on, to write them, to rewrite them, to continue writing them until our sisterhood loosens the lump of sand in my lungs. Did you feel them too?

20. Can we dance together, their words and my hips and these stories in this net we caught ourselves in?

21. Will the use of repetition ever make up for the loss of music?

22. When I say net, I mean the dredging up of us from the ocean of their ashes, my voice, and chutney music. Because I hardly have the power to avoid this clashing, but this changing and intertwining is the reality of chutney; or maybe I just like the mutilation of the men's voices who sing these songs?

23. I'm not that sadistic . . . right?

24. How can I tell you everything I've experienced in these verses and everything that is still missing?

Andre Bagoo

Translation is a reckoning with the impossible. What is language? Can language ever be "translated"? Can music ever be described? Can song be replicated on the page? Despite all of thin, or perhaps because of it, I wanted to find a different sense of musicality. I wanted stories, characters, arcs. At the same time, I didn't want to find them: I wanted them to remain embryonic ideas that were growing inside me, even if I sought to replicate a mood. I wanted to fly high like Icarus then lose my wings and spiral downwards. Rajiv Mohabir's glosses of these songs felt like narratives being telegrammed, awaiting discovery. Chutney might sometimes feel like an endless fete, but the authority of the symbolism here struck me, particularly in relation to the father figure. The mention of Kabir, whom I brought into service of one text, opened a line of inquiry for me that felt as though I'd walked into a magic closet. Translation is theft but it is also creation. I accepted, went with that.

It felt fitting, then, in coming up with my "original" responses, that I continue that sense of borrowing. I felt erasures of existing texts could suggest the syncopation of music, chutney's chops and jumps. I drew upon source material with a strong sense of patria, of colonial history, of indenture and slavery: Shakespeare's *The Tempest* and the first page of Samuel Selvon's *Turn Again Tiger* (his sequel to *A Brighter Sun*). Yet, even in this process of erasure, the earlier translations were echoed, etched as though I'd indeed fallen to the ground but was still looking up at the sun.

Anu Lakhan
Through the Music. And Through.

1. You must enter through the music. It is like a séance (listen to David Rudder's "Séance on the 6th and 7th Fret" from 2000's *Zero*), you will not always be allowed. Access sought must be granted willingly by what-if-who is on the other side. Any other way is barbarism.

2. "Āj Sawaliyā Sasur Ghar Jānā" and "Ham nā jāibe sasur ghar mē bābā" were probably more open to me than I deserve. Music is often good to me. Since I was not even allowed to play the triangle in the primary school band, music—knowing it had given me no gifts—gave me kindness. It was always near, and it introduced me to everything and everyone it knew. I am incapable of not falling in love with musicians, instruments, and individual songs.

3. Chutney and I have not always got on. I first heard both these songs the year two of my sisters got married and, since such behaviour (why would anyone get married? We have each other and our parents?) was anathema to me, I associated the nights of wedding chaos and strangers with Kanchan and Babla and the way they were taking my sisters away from me.

A dozen years later, marooned in Jamaica, I had my mother mail me the tape from that time. It was not yet stretched and unplayable. My father's beautiful, almost decorative handwriting was still clear. We had made our peace.

4. I lean in to brevity like a current. Instinctively and certainly. But working with these songs and working with the idea of translation wouldn't let me. My first drafts were like telegrams. After all, the songs were full of repetition and fluff about orhnis and domestic horrors. I could snap that neatly into a single sentence and it would all be so much tidier. I'd forgotten two things. The music, of course. But also

me. I'd forgotten that I was not editing. That there was another job I did that was not committed to reducing everything to a representative atom of sense. And so I walked back into the music.

5. How [really stretch your vocalization of the word into an agonized haaaaaaowwwwww] do these words match the music? Again, I am thinking not only of the originals, but the interpretations of others. Maybe, maybe "Āj Sawaliyā" could be a song of moderate seriousness Not "It occurs to me that I'm likely to die today," kind of serious, but it has some gravity. But "Ham nā jāibe" (referred to by childhood friends as "The Horsey Song" for the clip-clop intro of Babla's arrangement – and their assumption that this was the only reason I liked it, because of the horses), Ham nā jāibe is unspeakably gleeful. How can we take this poor girl, ever pursued by sticks and chores, seriously?

Are we meant to ignore the terribleness of going to one's in-laws— literally or metaphorically—because the message is delivered with a smile and a dance?

I wanted to dance. I wanted to whine my waist, curl up and screw the light bulb like never before. When the music hit me, I felt it in my bones, and nothing could stop me from moving in sync. Chutney music was the soundtrack to so much of my childhood. On many occasions, Sundar Popo played in my home—in my living room and even in my kitchen. I can remember my dad pulling out dusty vinyl from cardboard jackets and placing them onto his turntable in our South Bronx apartment whenever the family would visit. I didn't understand the words in the songs, but the infectious rhythm and melodic voices made me feel alive, made me feel joy.

As a teenager, I had learned about the history of chutney music and its significance in Indo-Caribbean culture. I was a student of the Rajkumari Cultural Center founded by Gora Singh and run by his sister, Pritha Singh. They were committed to preserving Indo-Caribbean arts & culture in NYC. Pritha often brought in older cultural custodians who taught us traditional wedding and birth (Sohar) songs along with their meanings. I learned that some of these very songs were the roots of those amazing chutney songs that made me want to move my waist. And I learned that it was women who sang these songs and passed them down generation after generation. Many of the songs also had spiritual undertones like "Nanda Baba" by Anand Yankaran for instance, but still had these upbeat tempos that your feet couldn't forget. All of this made me appreciate and love the music even more.

"Ham Nā Jāibe Sasur Ghar Mē Bābā" by Sundar Popo was a favorite wedding house tune for my family to curl up to. After taking in the literal translation of the song as a part of this process, I had to sit with some of the tension that it started to evoke within me. I recognize that the music has been and is in many ways a reflection of the way patriarchy shapes us as a people and is perpetuated in the values and norms we choose to hold onto. This is certainly the case with some of the newer chutney songs that revere drinking rum. However, I didn't have these feelings about chutney music in my childhood, when I held it on a higher pedestal. There was a playfulness, celebration, and nostalgia that I associated with it back then. In the translation of this particular Sundar Popo song, I felt it was important for me to tell a story from a young woman's point of view and not continue to perpetuate these patriarchal values. I wanted to show that her life had so much more meaning than just being a "data 'n law." I found it very straightforward to write the translation for this song because I knew the story that I wanted to tell.

The process for translating Yuseff Khan's song, "Āj Sawaliyā Sasur Ghar Jānā" was different. I wasn't familiar with it. I knew this song from the Babla & Kanchan cover, which was more of a dance track. Hearing this version of the song didn't surface any kind of special memories for me. Even though it was helpful to learn from the language gloss that "to go to one's father-in-law's house means to die/ go to God," it still took me some time to really reflect on and figure out what exactly this song was saying to me. I wasn't quite sure how I wanted to translate it. After re-reading it several times, I finally got inspired by the first line in the first verse "milengī saīyā," which literally means "will meet lover." The words poured out of me from that point on. I knew I wanted to tell a love story that spoke of a connection that continued even after death.

The themes that prevailed for me in both chutney song translations were grief and loss, and informed the direction I decided to take with the third poem. I decided to write in the vernacular of my parents, Guyanese creole, because I felt that it would help convey that chutney music energy by being authentic to the language and people the music birthed out of. I also wanted to tell the story of separation between two ancestors in my lineage—my great-great grandmother and my great-grandfather's brother.

Diving into the process of translating these two chutney songs and then writing my own original response was an exciting and creative challenge for me. It allowed me to reminisce on the important role chutney music has played in my life. It also allowed me to recognize that as much as I love and appreciate the music, there is still room for me to challenge and "push back" on the art form when it is not in alignment with my values. And I look forward to supporting more progressive chutney artists to hit the scene who can use their music to shift the culture of patriarchy in our community.

Anita Baksh

Dancing in the Parking Lot to *Tiny Winy*: Chutney, Feminism, and Diaspora

As a married Hindu Indo-Caribbean woman who lived for years with my in-laws, the verses of "Ham Nā Jāibe Sasur Ghar Mē Bābā" and "Āj Sawaliyā Sasur Ghar Jānā" deeply resonate with me as they foreground the traditional roles Indo-Caribbean women are often called upon to uphold, even today. The songs bring up sentiments of heterosexual patriarchal marriage as limiting one's freedom, agency, and desires and the idea that a woman leaves one's home and family behind to prioritize those of her husband. The alcoholism and domestic violence that pervade Indo-Caribbean households in the past and today, in the region and in the diaspora, are also present in these songs even if couched in subliminal and/or subversive language. Ironically, "Ham Nā Jāibe Sasur Ghar Mē Bābā" and "Āj Sawaliyā Sasur Ghar Jānā" are ingrained in my psyche through the voice and music of the Indian music duo: Kanchan (singer) and Babla (composer), not Indo-Caribbean male artists like Sundar Popo and Yusuff Khan who popularized them. Kanchan and Babla, a married couple from the Indian subcontinent, adapted songs from Sundar Popo and toured the Caribbean and other parts of the Indian diaspora singing chutney songs in the 1980s. Despite claiming that "it is their work in the chutney genre [rather than their contributions to Bollywood music] that Babla and Kanchan will really be remembered for," Rudradeep Bhattacharjee piece in *Scroll.in* magazine speaks little of the influence of the Indo-Caribbean diaspora on Babla and Kanchan's musical oeuvre and successful careers. An interesting case of how the diaspora impacts those on the "mainland" that disrupts narratives of a unilateral trajectory of influence.

My primary association with these chutney songs and Kanchan might be in part due to my age and my migration to the U.S. Perhaps it might also be an early sign of my feminist consciousness. My fondest memories of chutney music are related to songs sung by women: Kanchan, Atiya,[1] and Drupatee. This is ironic given that in the 1970s and 1980s when chutney became a popular genre of music, it was male dominated. Arguably this is still true today if we look at the Chutney Soca Monarch winners and household names like Ravi B. and Ki. Even though I am familiar with songs like "Maticore Night" and "Bhoonjay De Lawa", in my experience, popular women chutney artists, like sisters Hemlata "Hurricane" Dindial and Rasika Dindial, were not household names at that time. This is also an outcome of living in the diaspora where chutney music is not part of the national imaginary.

Regrettably, since I do not speak Bhojpuri or Hindi, I relied on the script provided in the project workbook and paired them with the sound of the music and the voices of the singers to guide my interpretations of these verses. The meaning of the words and their phonetic symbols on the page were unfamiliar, but their sounds and the voices who sang them resonate deep inside of me. First, I listened to Sundar Popo's and Yusuff Khan's versions, and then to the Kanchan and Babla versions of both. The tempo and beat of the latter are more fast-paced and vibrant than the others. The tune of the male songs are slow and somber, suggesting sadness and yearning. Listening to Kanchan's version allowed me to hear a subversive element of "Āj Sawaliyā Sasur Ghar Jānā." Rather than read the subject of the verse as a woman who is sad to leave her home, I believe that the term "beloved" can be read as a term of endearment used by a lover who is not her husband-to-be. The image of the stained veil supports this interpretation. The speaker of the song calls on his lover to accept that she is betrothed to someone else, perhaps as part of an arranged marriage. This interpretation challenges stereotypical images of Indian women as docile and submissive, without desire and sexual agency. The double meanings of song lyrics is an important element of the chutney tradition which originated as a part of the Maticore ceremony; a prelude to the Hindu wedding, these were the only spaces in which women sang songs and performed dances that covertly referenced sex acts, initiated and prepared brides for their wedding nights and marriage. Many of the songs Sundar Popo and Kanchan sang come from the Maticore and other communal spaces and represent songs that exist in a collective imaginary. A sole, originary author may not exist.

My fondest memory of listening to Kanchan is when I was about 5 years old in Guyana and my uncle took my sister and I to a concert at Rosehall Estate, Berbice. We lived with Mousa and Mousee (maternal aunt and her husband) while my parents ventured to New York City in search of work. They had tried their luck in Surinam but after having two little girls, they struggled to make it there as low-wage workers. When Kanchan performed in Guyana this time, my uncle couldn't afford tickets for the entire family, so we parked in the large parking lot adjacent to the fairground and stood on the hood of the car to watch the performance. We saw glimpses of small figures in shimmering outfits under bright lights on stage. The loud music and energy from the crowd made us feel like we were part of the paid audience. My sister and I danced in our colorful dresses, with layers of tulle wrapped around our waist, on the roof of the car to my favorite song at the time: "Tiny Winy." Even though a soca version existed, Kanchan's iteration was my favorite. I had rehearsed this moment many times at home, dancing on the coffee table in my underwear and short tank top with a ribbon tied across my forehead (like Indian starbai Mitum Chakraborty). As a young child I did not understand the economics of this moment, but was excited to be out at night partying and peeping for celebrities.

As I grew up in Jersey City and New York City, chutney music blared at wedding houses, maticores, and kangans as well as in cars and stores on Liberty Avenue and clubs like Tropics and Maracas (formerly Calypso City) in Queens. It didn't matter that the same songs were repeated each night. The hot songs ensured that the dance floors were packed. Wedding houses were also spaces where women expressed joy. In my newly immigrant working class family, women worked all the time: at the workplace as domestic workers (nannies, cleaners, and home health aides), and at home as caretakers, mothers, and wives. Wedding houses also required a lot of physical labor from family and friends. But that didn't stop anyone from enjoying the festivities. Women and children often occupied a separate part of the yard from the men who gathered together to drink and gyaff by the bar. But the dancefloor made these imaginary boundaries more porous. Women freely danced with each other, with children, and with partners. Men also danced with each other, displaying male bravado in the coiling of their wrists and gyrating of their waists, as they lowered their bodies down towards and up from the ground in unique and repetitive movements. In these moments, listening to and dancing to chutney was an important way to connect to "back home" and to express cultural identity in the diaspora.

ENDNOTES

1) In 1989, Atiya, who is originally from Holland, sang a cover of the Guyanese folk song, "Ke Ghunguru Doot Gaye." In the following year, she went on to do a cover of Mighty Trini's "Curry Tabanca."

2) Kangan is the third day of a Hindu Indo-Caribbean wedding ceremony where the couple removes the sacred thread tied around their wrists on the Maticore night. It is celebrated by the gathering of family and friends. For some, it also marks the day when the bride returns to her home for a week before finally joining her husband (and perhaps in-laws) for their new life together.

Elizabeth Jaikaran

I've always found the vocalizations in chutney music to sound like lamentations, notwithstanding watching waistlines roll and hips pelt to their recitation. Without knowing their meaning, perhaps some kind of linguistic intuition, passed on by some ancestor-turned-guardian-angel, told me that some of these most popular songs are really just a mourning placed on excited disco. Reading the literal translations of these songs was sobering and eureka all at once. In my poetic translation, it was crucial for me to retain the somberness of the content, almost as repentance for its decades of translation into wedding house jive and house party elation.

In my response poems, however, I crystallized a different goal for each of the songs. For "Hum Na Jaibay," my goal was to synthesize a post-wedding declaration of the narrator—a narration that both (a) follows up on her initial reactionary hysteria to the realization of her cruel unfathering and grim new home life, and (b) can be appended to the post-wedding narrative of many brides of toxic arranged marriages (historically and today). For "Aj Sawaliya Sasur Ghar Jana," on the other hand, my goal was to transpose the experience of loss and divinity in a way that I could smolder into emotion on paper in a reimagined way. While the original song seems to reference the loss of a spouse/lover, my response poem attempts to capture the same sentiments vis-à-vis the loss of a child, thus having the narrator reflect on her role as a creator, while also bowing to the majesty of the Creator. In this effort, I decided to break up a popular children's nursery rhyme in Guyana[1] into stanzas as a way of structuring grief and eventual healing through devotion, and thereby serving as the "stained veil" in this iteration of its retelling, with both the veil and rhyme as once pure, and now bleeding.

---

[1] I cannot say whether or not this nursery rhyme derives from Guyana, just that it is popular in Guyana.

Knock on the door (knock on the baby's forehead)
Peep in (touch the baby's eyes)
Turn the key (lightly twist the baby's nose)
Wipe your feet (brush the pointer finger under the baby's nose)
Walk in (walk two fingers along the baby's mouth)
Tell Mama Chin Chin, "morning!" (pinch the baby's chin playfully)

Ultimately, the exercise of metamorphosing these songs felt like a very intimate conversation with the past, with another world. In the course of that conversation, I was surprised to discover the timelessness of the sentiments expressed therein. And somewhere along this process, I realized that it was a seamlessness that almost made me want to dance. Arms out, and knees bent. With friends reunited after too much time apart.

Krystal M. Ramroop

For the Love of Chutney

Ingrained in me since small, my love for chutney music has always lured me to the dancefloor to break out in song—even if I was oblivious to the actual meaning of the lyrics—and "wuk my waistline" at Guyanese parties. In many efforts to dissect my identity in America, chutney music has even made me feel closer to my ancestors and my Indo-Caribbean heritage.

Steeped in rich Bhojpuri folk music, the vibrant and infectious genre of chutney serves as a bridge between the older and younger generations and the past, present, and future of the Indian diaspora. It also serves as a platform for the fusion of other genres, like calypso and soca. Chutney music signifies the preservation of traditions, linguistics, and rhythms—stemming from both traditional and modern instruments—from India to the Caribbean and abroad. In its exportation, the genre further allows boundaries to be broken in the reinvention of the quality of music produced within the diverse industry while raising awareness of and questioning the common normalizations and stigmas within Indo-Caribbean culture and the general Caribbean society and Indian diaspora.

In listening to and examining the evolution of chutney music and its lyrical poetry, evergreen themes rooted in religious rituals and hymns, family, relationships (whether it'd be ideal, forbidden, complicated, nonexistent), love, marriage, alcohol, women (bhauji is usually the "stargyal"), occupation and status, and reflections on migration, Caribbean life, and escapades—laced with segments of sexual innuendos as an ode to Bhojpuri music—motivate me to digest the importance of storytelling (even more as a storyteller myself!).

When translating the poetic compositions of "Ham Na Jaibe" and "Aaj Sawaliya" from chutney pioneers Sundar Popo and Yusuff Khan, respectively, I recognized their attention to the plight of the dulahin and the suffering she endures or will endure—both internally and externally—at her in-laws. However, while the bride professes to her father about the daily happenings between her mother and father-in-law—and why she isn't up to returning to their home—in Popo's song, the narrator in Khan's song urges the veiled bride to carry on with tradition despite the connotations evoked. This impacted my translation both literally and metaphorically as I considered how languages, practices, and ideologies were already intact but altered over time, location, and generations. I further contemplated the overall themes of gender ideologies and domestic violence in both the Indian diaspora and the Guyanese community, as well as the belief in India that husbands are Gods—known as pati parmeshwar.

All of this inspired a modern interpretation of my poem, "Bidaai." Throughout the poem, the bride is constantly acknowledged as beautiful. But while the opening stanzas emit an attractive, traditional sense of external beauty, the remaining stanzas challenge the bride's identity and the role she'll assume as she embarks on this new journey. There's also a subtle foreshadowing of how grim her life may be due to what may have already transpired internally (depression and anxiety) and what is to come as she leaves her family for another.

Nadia Misir

Confronting the translation gloss was like falling up a flight of stairs over and over again. I fell into a state of panic and unknowing. I wanted to "get it right," without realizing and appreciating that translation is writing and requires its own creative negotiations. I found myself asking so many questions. Do I put myself in the position of the singer who is really in the position of the bride to be married? Do I translate to standard American English or Guyanese-Creole? The negotiations felt like little lies, but are they really lies if the emotional truths—as complicated as they may be—still call out to us in each translation?

Chutney is hybrid for a reason. And while I grieved the loss of the languages my ancestors spoke, I felt deep gratitude for what grew out of language displacement and loss. I felt gratitude for the people doing the work of recovering our ancestral languages and making this accessible to our community. I felt joy at trying to grow an interpretation of these songs, to shape meaning where there was absence and blank space.

And while the stark lyrics of these songs are direct in the violence that awaits the bride, singing those lyrics does not change the outcome. The bride will go still. It seems like it doesn't matter how direct we are with communicating the atrocities and violence reserved for women, for anyone who does not clearly position themselves in the categories patriarchy has laid out like a tablecloth. Still blood flows. And we sing about it. Or maybe we sing despite it.

I grew up thinking about chutney songs as the soundtrack of celebrations. Songs that taught me how to whine up mi waist and throw my hands in the air. I didn't need to understand all of the lyrics to feel the way the music marked movement in my bones, the way a celebration song can map joy, but also grief and violence too. The deep wail of the singers' voices, the mournful sound of the harmonium, the upbeat tempo of the dholak—really, what does it mean for celebration songs to mark grief and violence too?

The first chutney song I distinctly remember hearing is "Lotela." I might have been four and five. The living room of the first house I grew up in on 109 avenue between 125 and 126 was transformed into a dance floor and our neighbors hadn't called the cops on us yet. An older uncle tried to lift my arms in the air, beckoning me to dance. I barked at him and ran up the stairs because I was what my relatives called touch-me-not and I wanted to sleep. I was annoyed that this old man I didn't recognize would try to force me to move my body. When I listen to chutney it never feels like the music is trying to take my body hostage. It feels more like prayer pulling at my limbs and bones.

Divya Persaud
Thoughts

Song 1: The lyrics are quite complex in showing the conflict between the mother- and father-in-law as well as between the subject and these people, and I resonated with the sense of being "frozen" amongst this conflict, particularly in how the lyrics repeat "daily" ("roj"). As always, my eye is drawn to the role of the woman in this song (although not to absolve her)—how she herself may be frozen. I was struck by the reference to adornment, which I've creatively interpreted, and wanted to emphasize this juxtaposition with the violence described in the song—and, generally, move from the subject's own frozen state to this fraught contrast between tenderness and violence for the woman.

From my use of the word "bejewels," I thought of how dust particles can "seed" clouds and lead to rain, or how crystals emerge deep in the earth, or out of magma, over long periods of time, beautiful but easily disappeared once again, leading to my original poem. These tiny particles are alone, caged, and frozen—in the midst of moving things have little agency.

Song 2: I really notice how in song and poetry from the subcontinent and West Indies, brides and women generally are used to signify death, and even here, her death is described through the dominance of men in her life. It made me think of how women are so integral and yet outside cultural imaginations, such that while nationhood is typically rendered as female, it is very much male. There's a lot that's nebulous and sublime here—at least in English—which enchanted me, particularly the reference to Kabir. I wanted to emphasize musicality in my translation and leave these references to Kabir and "jeers" without much further interpretation. In "pardes," I wanted to explore this outsider status of women through an almost vengeful lens, borrowing from the image of the kala pani.

Alex Bacchus
Translation Reflections

Chutney music is the Indo-Caribbean folk music I grew up listening to at family functions, and, coming into adulthood, chutney music has been a way to connect with my heritage and the Caribbean no matter how physically far away I may be. I have a soft spot for Surinamse singer Ashni Matadin's covers of "Bhool Bisar Mat Djana" and "More Garie Suno." Like many, but not all, anglo- and creolophone Indo-Caribbeans, I do not come from a home where South Asian languages are spoken. Listening to chutney music or even Bollywood songs in my coming of age, I usually never understood the true meaning of words. Over the years, I have studied Hindi and Urdu, and my vocabulary is greatly informed by cognates from my studies of Arabic, Farsi, Dari, Tajiki, and Turkish. Little by little, I have come to reconnect with the different musical genres of my childhood in a different way, and even more so with various current translation projects of Caribbean Hindustani lyrics. Learning their meaning, I see how much as anglo- and creolophone Indo-Caribbeans we are disconnected from the meanings of our beloved chutney music. I find it important to consider how this is similar to or different from the experiences of franco- and netherlandophone South Asian indenture descendants in the Caribbean and diaspora.

The Caribbean Hindustani lyrics of Trinbagonians Sundar Popo and Yusuff Khan and other chutney singers are different from the Urdu and Hindi I have studied and the language we commonly hear in Bollywood cinema, but at the same time similar. Caribbean Hindustani evolved in the Caribbean with the arrival of South Asian indentured labourers, who brought with them Bhojpuri, Awadhi, and other regional languages. Accessing the resources to learn South Asian languages considered more regional is generally difficult in North America. I cannot name definitively which languages my indentured ancestors spoke. Family mythologies may point to one direction and genealogical research to another with no concrete answer in either case. But my study of Hindi and Urdu is part of my greater passion for world languages, and, in studying language so much practice comes with textual translation. Applying those same skills, with study of Urdu-Hindi/Hindi-Urdu grammar and a lexical footing, one can dissect the lyrics, follow along, and even more so consulting dictionaries and Dr. Mohabir's provided glossary. Seeing the similarities between Caribbean Hindustani and Urdu and Hindi I find invigorating like the joy of putting jigsaw pieces together in solving a puzzle. I have always been excited by comparing languages, an interest beginning with the Romance languages in my early years.

Working on this project was one of the first times I investigated the meaning behind chutney lyrics with more intention, and I was not expecting to discover the songs' themes of gender-based violence (GBV) and alcoholism. I was particularly intrigued to discover the feminist resistance in Popo's male-sung "Ham Nā Jāibe Sasur Ghar Mē Bāba" with the lyric I translate as "meh nah guh go." GBV and alcoholism are issues Caribbean people do not commonly discuss, and Sundar Popo's male voice singing a woman' lines of refusal surprised me. However, feminist resistance is no oddity in Caribbean music or the region as a whole, and we can find many examples across dancehall, soca, zouk, reggaeton, and more, even though the genres may be commonly conceived as patriarchal. The timeline of starting this project coincided with my Hindi class discussing depictions of women in Bollywood item numbers during my undergraduate study abroad at SOAS, University of London. And this led me to further interrogate anglophone Indo-Caribbean consumption of our non-English and non-Creole song lyrics. What do songs do for us?

I turn to the words of bell hooks in reflecting on the chutney lyrics and common social issues in Caribbean communities:

men who oppressed women did not do so because they acted simply from the space of free will; they were in their own way agents of a system they had not put into place. Yet our compassion for patriarchy's abuse of men was not as intense as our passion for female agency and our will to gain social equality with men.[1]

With the themes of GBV; societal gender roles, expectations, and pressures; and alcoholism, we need to look holistically to heal these harms our society continues to carry. In healing women, femmes, and gender diverse kin, we need to also heal our men. And in translating our music, how can we see and understand better the structures and systems of gender, race, and power we live within? How did they start? How are they rewritten and remade? Where and how do we listen to chutney? How has that changed with time and what did that look like in the past?

I carry the memory of listing to Babla and Kanchan's cover of "Ham Nā Jāibe Sasur Ghar Mē Bāba" as a young child at a family event, an overall joyous atmosphere with the song's upbeat rhythm. A common anglophone Indo-Caribbean experience involves consuming chutney and Bollywood songs without fully understanding them; of course, that is not the case for all. These songs have their own meaning to us as part of our Indo-Caribbean culture. But we enjoy these songs without knowing their significance or having the chance to be critical, and this is a product of our colonial and post-colonial journey and making, just like the conditions that created the subjectivities many of these songs recount. Yet, it is also important to make space for reconciliation of these lyrics' meanings on top of solely understanding translations. In part, this is to reconcile our coolieness or coolietude. This is to reconcile our own livings written from and within colonialism, patriarchy, racism, misogyny, transqueerphobia, ableism, and other harmful systems too.

In the majority of the anglophone Caribbean, Caribbean Hindustani registers are at risk of disappearance, and, even today in South Asia, pressures of speaking English or another dominant language like Hindi create risks for regional languages like Bhojpuri and Awadhi. Meeting Dr. Mohabir was my first time meeting a Guyanese speaker of the language I had many questions about in

[1] hooks, 34.

childhood, a language my family and I could only imagine. In some ways, these languages were stolen from our ancestors in becoming Caribbean and being displaced from South Asia. However, we cannot forget today's few speakers and their narratives either. In translating Sundar Popo's "Ham Na Jaibe Sasur Ghar Mē Bāba" and Yusuff Khan's "Aj Sawaliyā Sasur Ghar Jānā," it was crucial for me to produce lyrics comprehensible to the Guyanese and Trinbagonians part of my early life, and this was also a task serving to promote and give greater significance to our English-based Creoles and our creolized identities. While our Creoles are often somewhat intelligible to English speakers, I intentionally chose Creole over English because of the lack of attention our language receives, and the ideology of our Creoles limited to the common phrasing of "broken English" or "brukkup English," sentiments learned in our colonial experience from classism, ableism, racism, anti-Blackness, and white supremacy. "Folk" means "people." Folk music is music of the people, and di peepl bina takk Kreeyoleez.

Neither we nor our languages are broken. Understanding the meanings and origins of both Creoles and English gives deeper meaning to who we are as people. My own verses of poetry blend my Creole and English the way we talk. In translating, some words I selected may be closer to their literal translation and others may be added or changed to evoke sentiment, affective charge, or greater connection. Writing in Guyanese Creole, I face the uniqueness of writing language without standardized spellings. In writing English-based Creoles, we may have the same or similar phrases, but we are almost guaranteed to have different spellings, even across my own works, and this is something I find beautiful about our languages. The two Caribbean songs revolve around a dialogue about a young woman resisting going to her in-laws' and another pushing the resisting persona to go. My responsibility as a translator is to uplift these dialogues, and so much of language also lives in song passed down from one generation to another. Having lived most of my life in North America, my own register of Creole is specific to the time and location of my family's origins in the countryside of Guyana's East Coast Demerara, the historical lands of the Dutch Demerary and later the British Demerara sugar colony.

With my time spent in the Caribbean, I have come to notice how my language differs from today's domestic speakers and how my language changes while listening to and speaking with them.

There is undeniably much more meaning to chutney music to discover and unpack, and these translation experiences warn of the work it takes to actively be critical and aware of our different music and to nuance and complicate our understanding of our culture and society, something that is not accessible to all Caribbean people in the region or in diaspora. This work requires many privileges. However, not all art has to be political, and people deserve to find joy in the music of our upbringings. But for those seeking to understand and unpack that what is echoed through artistic artifacts like chutney songs, there is much, much complexity. Moving forward, it is imperative we do not forget the resistance of the past when considering the social injustices in the Caribbean and Caribbean diasporas. In doing so, we can learn from each other, our siblings, and neighbours. The diaspora can and needs to learn from the current domestic Caribbean, and we can continue these traditions of subversion and resistance by writing new lyrics, making music, and producing art relevant to our contemporary experiences in our own challenging of the status quo. And, simultaneously, we can celebrate and record the various registers of the Caribbean's Creoles, and give greater status, meaning, and recognition to our language, identity, and personhood as well.

WORKS CITED

hooks, bell. *Communion: The Female Search for Love.*
William Morrow, 2002.

Miranda Rachel Deebrah

Dancing in Dualities

Put on a chutney song and me guh dance! Wedding house, backyard family gatherings, alone in my room—regardless of occasion or setting, I will dance. I am visited by a memory of my 5-year-old self who once attended the wedding of a cousin in Success Village along Guyana's East Coast, and spent most of the day timidly trailing after my parents. That is, until the first notes of "Chutney Bacchanal" filled the bottom house where the wedding reception took place. Suddenly, I was on the dance floor in a heartbeat, whining up my waist as though I came out the womb dancing. Gone were my inhibitions, replaced by an innate boldness and fiery spirit that came alive with the sweet sounds of chutney. Chutney inexplicably draws me to the dance floor; it is an indelible part of who I am. To me, chutney sounds and feels like home. It feels like part of my very lifeblood, representing a mashup of my dual Indianness and Caribbeanness and all that comes with it. Chutney's presence is eternal in my community, at family functions and, of course, back home in Guyana every day. It is as much of a proud and undeniable legacy of Indian Indenture as I am.

Yet, I was hardly prepared for what I encountered during this process of translating "Ham Na Jaibe" and "Aaj Sawaliya," specifically the lyrical content pertaining to marriage, gender violence, and sexism against women, previously unknown to me, given my inability to understand the Bhojpuri language. What struck me most was the intrinsic hybrid nature of chutney songs wherein light, upbeat tempos are juxtaposed against a backdrop of thematically dark subject matters, which we readily dance to without true understanding. In a way, this contrast of music and lyrics in chutney composition—as well as our community's fond relationship with chutney despite the loss of our ancestral language, which renders us incapable of grasping the meanings of these songs without aid—reemphasized the natural hybridity and duality of origins that chutney represents for me and how I perceive my complex Indo-Caribbean identity.

It wholly shifted my perception of chutney, as I now contemplate it with a newfound insight as music that is far more than just lively tunes to mindlessly dance to and which holds deeper meaning beneath the surface. The ties to indenture are even more clear and push me to think further about my own role, as a descendant, in shaping the ongoing legacy of our heritage. Particularly interesting is the revelation that for a cultural community that is notoriously silent on the topic of gender violence and related issues, we are somehow able to openly address it in song, although masked behind a language that slips further away from us with each passing generation. Perhaps chutney was and is a means to confront such heavy topics in its ability to provide enough artistic distance through its carefree, rhythmic beats and a now-foreign tongue which grants us safety to face our unpleasant truths which are anything but carefree. Through chutney, the plight of the Indo-Caribbean woman becomes an open secret. More complexity, more duality.

My translation efforts and original poem thus reflect this theme of inherent duality I repeatedly encountered. I aimed to translate not just the actual words but also the ideas and overall feeling of the songs using both my native Guyanese Creolese dialect and standardized English via a spoken word poetic style. Each line is penned with deliberate rhythm and cadence in mind, with the overall pieces written with the intention of infusing within them the sing-songy musicality of our precious Creolese, and ensuring they were "performance-ready"— extensions of the original songs themselves. Faith coloured my approach; the first translation is interpreted and written as a pleaful prayer from the unnamed speaker's perspective, while the second is meant to resemble a religious hymn or a passage from scriptures imparting a sacred yet somber message.

My own poem responds to both, directly addressing the forlorn speaker of the first song—who I think of as a sister, my Jahaji Bahin— to give her, and by extension my sisters of the diaspora, a new message that counters that of the latter song. It attempts to both move away from the melancholic themes of traditional chutney music and change the painful narrative that has followed Indo-Caribbean women since the dawn of our existence to one filled with hope and empowerment, thus solidifying my commitment to seeking justice and healing for all my sisters. It is to say, this legacy of violence and suffering will end.

Will Depoo

Both chutney songs discuss relationships to in-laws. Being forced to go to your in-laws. In Sundar Popo's song, I kept hearing a woman's voice, saying *I don't want to go.* She's describing the alcoholism, abuse, and surveillance of the in-laws. In Yousef Khan's song, I imagine someone, or several, is telling a woman she must go to her father-in-law. And, if Khan's song believes that to go to the in-laws is to die, then it seems she's told she must be with god, she must die. To me, the song is implying her husband is dead, and she has to join him.

With this in mind, I translated both thinking about the control exerted over women. She has to go her in-laws, she has to have a stained veil. So, I wrote a poem to counter the patriarchy in those songs. She shouldn't have to deal with abusive and disrespectful in-laws. Being married doesn't mean she has to poojay her in-laws. Many women experience similar situations in our community. At Hindu weddings, they become very emotional with "giving away" the bride to in-laws. It doesn't seem like a union, it seems like a sentence. We can do the religious practices, but do we have to follow traditions? Or, can we shift the tradition?

A chutney singer and song I was thinking about to counter the narratives in these songs is Drupatee and her song "Daru." Drupatte's music counters the narrative that women must be subordinate and traditional. "Daru" speaks about drinking rum by "Cora River." While it's changing, it is still taboo for women to publicly drink, and when they are at bars, many times they experience sexual harassment. And, the women workers at these parts are treated very poorly by the customers, almost all men. So, a song like "Daru" challenges these notions of who can drink.

Kaneesha Cherelle Parsard

Across the two chutney songs, I knew only one of the Hindi/ Caribbean Hindustani words I was to translate: ghar, or home.

Ghar is a term that travels. It can be found in the discourses of the late-nineteenth-century Indian anti-colonial nationalists: Their vision was one that split the *ghar*—the domestic sphere, in which women would guard cultural and spiritual life—and the bahir—from public sphere in which men would lead the newly *independent* state and integrate it into the West.[1] In this view, an independent India would be forged by sequestering women.[2] Across the kala pani, the Indians who made lives as indentured labor in the Caribbean and the Indian Ocean world used the concept of the ghar, and its gendered meanings, to make sense of their circumstances. Indo-Guyanese-American writer Gaiutra Bahadur's research reveals that the "coolie" barracks were sometimes known as kasbi ghar, or brothels.[3] Though women were recruited in low numbers, the exploitation of "coolie" women came to shape the very vocabulary of indentured laborers.

As the ghar moves, it contains violence and the warmth of the familiar all at once. No wonder that this is the metaphor of the *nirgun*: as our convener Rajiv Mohabir reminds us, "to go to one's in-laws" is to die or to go to God. It travels across genre and form as well as across geography. I was reminded of our best-known Caribbean protagonist of Indian descent: Mohun Biswas. In V.S. Naipaul's *A House for Mr Biswas* (1961), Biswas' life begins in earnest only when he leaves the *sasur ghar*, the home of the Tulsis.[4] Sung no less than six times across the two chutney songs—in Sundar Popo's 1979 track, the opening line

---

[1] Partha Chatterjee, "The Nationalist Resolution of the Women's Question (1989)," in *Empire and Nation: Selected Essays* (New York: Columbia University Press, 2010), 116–35.
[2] Inderpal Grewal, *Home and Harem: Nation, Gender, Empire and the Cultures of Travel* (Durham, N.C.: Duke University Press, 1996), 54.
[3] Gaiutra Bahadur, *Coolie Woman: The Odyssey of Indenture* (Chicago: University of Chicago Press, 2013), 84.
[4] V.S. Naipaul, *A House for Mr. Biswas* (London: Andre Deutsch Ltd., 1961).

("Ham na jaibe sasur ghar me baba") seems to repeat ad infinitum—
the ghar became the central trope of my translation.

But the warmth and violence of the ghar, and of domesticity,
literally sounds different than it might be read. Sundar Popo joyfully
and yet insistently sings his speaker's refusal. I wondered how to
translate its tone and temporality. Would the line speak for itself
on the page or would I lose the force of refrain? In the end, I opted
for economy and intensity over repetition. To capture this sense of
possibility in the first two lines, I settled on "I turn my back on my
in law's door." If one freezes in the home of one's in-laws ("Jiyara jar
gail hamar baba"), one might also be reanimated when escaping their
grasp. And there is reason to turn away: the abuse, toward the speaker
and toward the mother-in-law, is so regular that it might be scheduled.
With each day, violence punctuates what should be a refuge.

Not everyone can refuse. In Yousef Khan's song, I translated the
titular line ("Āj sawaliyā sasur ghar jānā") as "It is your time." The
English-language idiom conveyed the line's inevitability. Whether
one can choose to go to one's in-laws or not seems a matter of gender
difference: the oppositional speaker in Popo's song could be a man,
while in Khan's song the finality (along with the reference to veils)
suggests that its addressee is a woman. Though she is without choice,
the song has a tenderness: I added the call of beti, or daughter.

As I thought about my hopes for Khan's addressee, I wondered:
What is the narrative alternative to these nirgun? Where might one
go, if not to one's in-laws or to God? If one refuses domesticity, might
one never die?[5] This is not merely a conceptual question as, more
than a century after the end of indenture, Indo-Caribbean women in
the region and in the diaspora continue to die at the hands of their
partners. To shift the line in my second translation: "Beti, where will

[5] Here, I follow the insights of Suzanne Persard who insists upon an understanding of chutney as "a
site of subversive sexualities within the context of empire and (post-)indentureship" in "Queering
Chutney: Disrupting Heteronormative Paradigms of of Indo-Caribbean Epistemology," *Journal
of West Indian Literature* 26, no. 1 (April 2018). See also Tina Campt, "Black Visuality and the
Practice of Refusal," *Ampersand, Women & Performance* (blog), February 25, 2019, https://
www.womenandperformance.org/ampersand/29-1/campt. I am also thinking with Tina Campt
and the Practicing Refusal collective, whose work in Black studies and in Black feminist studies
interrogates how artists wield "negation" against anti-Black violence.

you go instead?" We might make a home not in the mundane violence of the domestic, but rather in the *wild*. I think, in a final intertextual gesture, of Indo-Guadeloupean artist Kelly Sinnapah Mary's wild visual practice in *Notebook of No Return*.[6] In one image from the collection, the central figure is reticent, wearing a mask. At the same time, she is excessive: her braids grow downward and then through the fence that surrounds her. So, to turn away from the domestic is both to refuse patriarchal dominance in the home but also to refuse enclosure as a strategy of imperialism and of the plantation. My original poem, "The Coolie Woman Climbs Out of the Portrait," takes up this hope.

If an island is a world, so too is the ghar. The gender violence in Sundar Popo's song cannot be disentangled from the violence of Western modernity at large. Seeking the wild is a call to invert these logics. To repair, from the home to enclosures of all kinds, the violence of Indigenous dispossession, of chattel slavery, of Asian indentureship.[7]

---

[6] Kelly Sinnapah Mary, *Notebook of No Return*, 2018, Painting on paper, 240 cm x 140 cm, 2018. For an elaboration of Sinnapah Mary's visual approach, see Andil Gosine, "Désir Cannibale: Kelly Sinnapah Mary's *Notebook of No Return*," *Asian Diasporic Visual Cultures and the Americas* 5, no. 1–2 (April 11, 2019): 11–30, and Lisa Outar, "Art, Violence, and Non-Return: An Interview with Guadeloupean Artist Kelly Sinnapah Mary," in *Indo-Caribbean Feminist Thought: Genealogies, Theories, Enactments,* eds. Gabrielle Jamela Hosein and Lisa Outar, New Caribbean Studies (New York: Palgrave Macmillan US, 2016), 193–202.
[7] This is an expression of the "relational difference" that anthropologist Shanya Cordis advocates for in "Forging Relational Difference: Racial Gendered Violence and Dispossession in Guyana," *Small Axe: A Caribbean Journal of Criticism* 23, no. 3 (60) (November 1, 2019): 18–33.

Afterword

Chutney Feminist Poetics: The Politics and Possibilities of Post-Indenture Coolie Grammars

—

Ryan Persadie
(Women and Gender Studies, University of Toronto)

In her foundational essay "Poetry Is Not a Luxury," Audre Lorde directs our attention to the power of prose and the pedagogies of memory, resistance, and survival that poetics holds. For her, poetry is both archive and counter-archive, figurative and material, a potential and a praxis, a method of feeling in the now and sensing into the then. Poetry operates as a critical grammar of care-work and resurgency, a strategy of assembling fragments, histories, and traces of emotional and affective archives that have been subjugated to colonial duress and epistemological debris.

Poetry helps minoritarian truth leak out of the porous tombs of submerged and stratified positionings of subaltern knowledge. It operates as a means of reading into the violences of the past, a technology of contending with the realities of the present, and a teleological pursuit to architect worlds outside of contemporary hegemonic realities. The poetic helps us contend with the affective sensibilities of everyday and historical violence, where all of us begin to feel the crushing weight of systemic power. It is first through poetry that decolonial agitators can contend with an emerging repertoire, praxis, and methodology of finding, building, and architecting language to make sense of the unjust world in which we live.[1] As Lorde writes, poetry and the cultivation of poetics, particularly for marginalized subjects, is:

> A vital necessity of our existence. It forms the quality of the light within which we predicate our hopes and dreams towards survival and change, first made into language, then into idea, then into more tangible action.[2]

As Sarah Ahmed further develops, "feminism is sensational" and it is only first through feeling the material and intergenerational articulations, residues, and viral pollutants of colliding injustices that we can begin to build grammar for decolonial (un/de/re)worlding practices, or otherwise what to she refers to as positioning oneself as the "feminist killjoy."[3] Poetry helps us conjugate old imperial tongues and historical materialities towards dialects of contemporary anti-colonial knowing and future building. Such translation operates through interstitial archives of what poet Derek Walcott has referred to as "buried language" and the "natural and the marmoreal" whereby vocalities of ontological re-making and transformation can emerge.[4] Poetics has offered us the necessary mechanisms to pursue that call. As Lorde teaches us:

> There are no new pains. We have felt them all already. We have hidden the fact that in the same place where we have hidden our power. They lie in our dreams, and it is our dreams that point the way to freedom. They are made realizable through our poems that give us the strength and courage to see, to feel, to speak, and to dare.[5]

The poetic provides us with repertoires of instinctive and insurgent

---

[1] Ahmed, *Living a Feminist Life.*
[2] Lorde, "Poetry," 37.
[3] Ahmed, *Living a Feminist Life.*
[4] Walcott, "The Antilles."
[5] Lorde, "Poetry," 37.

urgency that allow us to articulate "injustice, to recover lost values, to bring change, to remain sane" and to breathe vocality into that which is otherwise unspeakable.[6] Radical poetics contends with histories of empire and conquest through acts of critically re-making language, where the word and tongue of the colonial past can be re-configured to work towards disaggregating and pursuing a decolonial present.

Afro-Jamaican feminist scholar Hazel Carby specifically reminds us how strategies of emancipatory self-making began in language.[7] In contending with their historiographies and translations, we work toward narrating the harms and struggles of our lives as we come face-to-face with the genealogies of their birthing. For instance, to understand the imperial force of language we must fully comprehend how acts of writing—particularly legislation, codification, and cartography—first provided colonial forces with the mechanisms to conquer. Our first planetary systems of social and ontological stratification worked through the establishment of marked visible lines, scripts, and notes that crafted marked zones of territory and (non)/human emplacement.[8] Through codifying observations of colonial seeing and sensing, imperial power was first weld through the technologies of language that worked to categorize hemispheric categories of human and nonhuman, modern and primitive, the enslaved and indentured, the bourgeois and the poor.

Drawing us back to the the temporal birthplace of Western categories of power (such as race, class, gender) and liberal humanism, we can understand how European Enlightenment-era ideals that produced such regimes of hegemonic normativity and empire were only made possible through the work of accountable subjects and the language work they pursued. In her public lecture entitled "Imperial Sexual Economies," Carby traces how genres of humanity were crafted through calligraphy, particularly through the pen and ink of colonial bureaucrats, accountants, and colonial managers. Codifying classifications of superiority and inferiority through marking land, legislation, and physical bodies instilled settler colonial power over the

---

[6] Ali, "Poetry," 6.
[7] Carby, "Imperial Sexual Encounters."
[8] Carby, "Imperial Sexual Encounters."

lives and histories of the subaltern. Through such material linework, they were able to pursue colonial projects that used regulatory strategies by gridding voluminous space, not only attempting to paint worlds through the cultivation of rigid divisions of human belonging and emplacement, but also working towards holding their ethno-nationalist claims to it. Situated within a landscape of colliding pandemics of brutality, violence, and (both physical and ontological) injury that emerge from such a settler colonial project, poets working from subjectivities of marginality—and particularly those of the Global South—have demonstrated how mechanisms enforced upon the lives of the colonized and their descendants, such as language and writing, can be expanded, extended, fragmented, and brought together again to coalesce into new transgressive vocalities.

Such forms of multiplicity, ecological transformation, and re-imagining have always been intrinsic to the genealogy of the Caribbean as a birthplace of contemporary globalization, mixture, and heterogeneity. Produced through conflicting vectors of difference, culture, power, and human emplacement, Caribbean poetics have shown us the potentials and possibilities that re-invention have brought forward in producing important feminist languages to resist logics of rigid, static, fixed, and normative place and time. The emergence of creole, patois, and other hybrid Caribbean languages that descend out of what Lisa Lowe refers to as the "intimacies of four continents" is perhaps one of the most obvious examples of the transformative potential of acts of re-making colonial technologies.[9] Working through the politics of perversion (which I extend upon from the work of Ariane Cruz),[10] we see how the site of an irrational, illegible, illicit, and pejorative archive of that which was not supposed to exist becomes the epistemological center by which transgressive knowledge can be made.

To speak outside of the violent archive of tyrannical normativity, Caribbean poets have worked through such feminist methodologies of re-invention via translation to contend with the ecological parameters,

[9] Lowe, *Intimacies.*
[10] Cruz, *Colour of Kink.*

subjectivities, and struggles that Caribbean life has produced. More specifically, autobiography, standpoint, and biomythography (as conceptualized by Audre Lorde) have been a core technology in Caribbean feminist poetic traditions to craft literary genealogies that re-work the queer archive of Caribbeanness to build language to speak the self, unsettle (settler) colonial logics of white supremacy and its consequential offspring, and furthermore evidence how the subaltern *can* speak. For instance, writer Toni Morrison specifically notes how Euro-American thinkers such as Immanuel Kant, Thomas Jefferson, and David Hume crafted racialized notions of rationality as only accessible to those carrying class, masculine, and white supremacist power while simultaneously positioning Black communities, and specifically the enslaved and their descendants, of incapable of writing critical theory and prose.[11] For minoritarian communities, poetry and writing thus can never be understood as "luxury"; they are always a critical tool of knowledge creation, memory-holding, space-creating, and imaginative feminist and decolonial world-making.

I Will Not Go is a transnational and intergenerational archive of locationg Indo-Caribbean translation, and grammar to speak Coolie selfhoods across struggle, geography, and time. Speaking through the afterlife of indenture, the contributors work through the crossings of Indian and Atlantic ocean worlds, between intersecting routes that move in non-linear trajectories, forming queer circuitries that shift across what we now call South Asia, the Caribbean, and the diaspora to find insurgent voice. Through embodied methodologies of resonance, translation, reverberation, appropriation, and re/de-memorialization, chutney song and dance forms are re-mixed and re-configured with contemporary diasporic consciousness to cultivate a distinct set of chutney feminist poetics.

My reading of chutney feminist poetics largely draws upon the work post-indentureship feminist archives that have worked to re-claim Indo-Caribbean selfhoods outside of logics of pain, trauma, and dislocation as well as craft embodied languages to speak to contemporary decolonial pursuits that move through the histories,

[11] Morrsion, "Site of Memory," 2.

163

legacies, and social movements of the descendants of indenture. In working to craft language to speak to indentured pasts and translate decolonial coolie presents, the work of translation here pursues feminist calls first set out by Indo-Caribbean gender scholars and activists Gabrielle Hosein and Lisa Outar in their edited collection *Indo-Caribbean Feminist Thought*. In line with their arguments, we see coolie feminist poetics following genealogies of post-indentureship feminisms that:

> draw on Indo-Caribbean diasporic cosmologies, artifacts, archetypes, myths, symbols, engagements with embodiment, popular cultural expressions, the sacred and the sexual, and intellectual traditions and concepts to articulate a feminist praxis where Indian gendered experiences in the Caribbean are not marginal, while being understood in ways centered in a politics of solidarity across ethnicity, class, gender, sexualities, and nation.[12]

Turning to genres of chutney performance and the pedagogies of post-indentureship feminisms they offer also helps us interrogate the transgressive grammars this anthology provides. Coalesced through the crossings of Indian and Atlantic Ocean world cultures, the archive of chutney begins through a genealogy of non-normative difference. Echoed to us through the vocalities of indentured melismas, distinctly coolie instrumentations, and jahaji-bhai/n pedagogies, chutney emerges within a framing of newly emerging subjectivity, ontology, and experience that was only made possible through following the contours of Indo-Caribbean labour histories and migrations.

Facing the brunt of this wrath, the traditional arbiter of this sacred song and dance form, or the figure of the coolie woman, was positioned as abnormality both in colonial India and emerging Caribbean nationalisms. Irrecuperable within framings of respectable Brahmanic womanhood, British Victorian femininity, emerging neoliberal women subjecthoods based in Christian moral groundings,

---

[12] Hosein and Outar, "Introduction," 3.

and emerging national Creole sensibilities, she was largely upheld, as famously noted by Mahatma Gandhi, as a "broken vessel" and part of a larger "hostile and recalcitrant minority" (as Eric Williams expressed) whose brokenness, fragmentation, and ruptured genealogy positioned her to an always-already non-normative elsewhere.

Chutney soundworlds—which begin with the emergence of a coolie woman subjectivity birthed through the expulsion from multiple state, imperial, and local ontological apparatuses—provide us with critical understandings to locate Coolie knowledge through its birthing through difference and inscribe the art form with transgressive power as it sounds and orchestrates energies of the decolonial *free up*. We must be clear not to connote my reading of Coolie subjectivity as different from the diasporic trauma archive that traditional Indo-Caribbean studies has been largely consumed with. In its articulations, this was often seen through writings concerned with finding a seat at the identitarian Creole and South Asian table. Such kala pani subjectivities and the injury diasporic Coolie communities faced through their displacements from the "authentic" homeland of India operated to position our ontologies through ongoing (nationalist) irreparability and non-belonging. However, what would it mean to refuse such nationalist aspirations of identity validation? How do we instead build an archive of Coolie feminist knowing not only via trauma, pain, and woundedness, but through sites and routes of pleasure, erotics, and transgressive self-making (as Coolie people have always done)? What does a resurgence of Coolieness from its genealogical birthplace—the site of non-conformity, of queerness, of the ruptured—provide for us as a critical transnational poetics of self?

The contributors to this volume have helped us to pursue this critical pedagogical praxis. Engaged in methods of experimentation, translation, re-mixture, and conjugation—technologies of which produced what we now call the Indo-Caribbean in the first place— we are provided with new epistemological sensoria to re-spatialize, -orient, and -imagine coolie lifewords through cultivation of language, grammar, and vocality. With chutney as a initial pedagogical center, we are able to think more critically through the sensibilities of indentured pasts, Indo-Caribbean presents, and Coolie futures, and to make sense of an archive that has largely only been available to us through traces, glimmers, traces, and colonial tools of excavation.

Through cultivating methods and archives that work through these pedagogies of queerness, difference, mobility, the embodied, and the non-normative, we understand how spaces, histories, and subjectivities that emerge from what we now understand as the "Indo-Caribbean" have always been imbued with transgressive action, configuration, and disruptive potential and agency. Extending important theorizations offered to us by Ann Stoler, we think about how archives of feminist and decolonial Indo-Caribbean epistemology have been affected by processes of relentless imperial force and other conditions "induced by illegitimate pressure."[13] Or, as Tao Leigh Goffe powerfully argues, how such pressures work through "archives of digestion" or what she calls the "politics of gastropoetics": a process of knowledge survival and death that work through historical and contemporary processes that dictate "who gets absorbed and incorporated into history" and who gets "left undigested" by the (neo)colonial world.[14]

However, these imperial acts of deliberate erasure, despite their colonial strength, have not resulted in the erasure or the extinction of subaltern knowledge. On the contrary, the obstructions placed against minoritarian ways of theorizing submerged feminist selfhoods have pushed us into cultivating new ways of sensing their teachings as we strain to feel, hear, and read differently in the world and, in doing so, re-frame "our capacities to re-vision . . . what we imagine already to know," as Stoler has declared. This collaborative project helps us to lean into Indo-Caribbean vocalities that have been subject to both historical and ongoing imperial processes that have "saturated the subsoil" of our lives through the ruination of non-normative social being. Yet, despite such technologies of suffocation, *I Will Not Go* helps us think about the formidability of such queer archives and the voluminous fluid forms they have taken to be able to speak and teach differently.

[13] Stoler, *Duress.*
[14] Goffe, "Sugarwork."

BIBLIOGRAPHY

Ahmed, Sarah. *Living a Feminist Life*. Durham: Duke University Press, 2017.

Ali, Nosheen. "Poetry, Power, Protest: Reimagining Muslim Nationhood in Northern Pakistan." *Comparative Studies of South Asia, Africa, and the Middle East* 32, no 1 (2012): 13-24.

Carby, Hazel. "Imperial Sexual Economies." Public Lecture, University of Toronto, Canada, November 18, 2020.

Cruz, Ariane. *The Colour of Kink: Black Women, BDSM, and Pornography*. New York: NYU Press, 2016.

Goffe, Tao Leigh. "Sugarwork: The Gastropoetics of Afro-Asia After the Plantation." *Asian Diasporic Visual Cultures and the Americas* 5 (2019): 31-56.

Hosein, Gabrielle, and Lisa Outar, eds. "Introduction." In *Indo-Caribbean Feminist Thought: Genealogies, Theories, Enactments*, 1-20. New York: Palgrave MacMillan, 2016.

Lorde, Audre. "Poetry Is Not a Luxury." In *Sister Outsider: Essays and Speeches*, 36-39. Berkeley: Crossing Press, 1985.

Lowe, Lisa. *The Intimacies of Four Continents*. Durham: Duke University Press, 2015.

Morrison, Toni. "The Site of Memory." In *Inventing the Truth*, edited by William Zinsser, 1-4. New York: Houghton Mifflin Company, 1995.

Stoler, Ann. *Duress: Imperial Durabilities in Our Times*. Durham: Duke University Press, 2016.

Walcott, Derek. "The Antilles: Fragments of Epic Memory." Nobel Prize in Literature Lecture, 1992. https://www.nobelprize.org/prizes/literature/1992/walcott/lecture/.

Contributors

ALEX BACCHUS is a hyperpolyglot and multidisciplinary artist of Guyanese and Sicilian origin. They studied International and Global studies at Middlebury College and are studying Communication Studies at McGill University. As a language lover, Alex studied Persian and Persianate cultures as a Fulbright fellow in Dushanbe, Tajikistan, in addition to the Romance languages, several Caribbean creoles, Arabic, Hindi, Urdu, and other languages. Their creative writing and artistry are informed by their intersectional journey in life and inherited lineage narratives. Through their linguistic, cultural, and historical curiosity, they find great inspiration from understanding the heterogeneous makeup of today's Caribbean and Latin America and seeing just how much the Caribbean Sea connects the region's people more so than it separates.

ANDRE BAGOO is a Trinidadian poet and writer. His publications include the poetry collection *Narcissus* (Broken Sleep Books, 2022), the short fiction sequence *The Dreaming* (Peepal Tree Press, 2022) and the essay collection *The Undiscovered Country* (Peepal Tree, 2020). His latest work is the poetry collection *Midnight Bestiaries* (Broken Sleep, 2024).

ANITA BAKSH was born in Surinam, lived in Guyana and Trinidad, and grew up in New York City. She received her Bachelor's from St. John's University and her Ph.D. from the University of Maryland, College Park. She is Professor of English at LaGuardia Community College, City University of New York (CUNY). Her publications on Indo-Caribbean literature and culture appear in such outlets as the *The Journal of West Indian Literature* and *Indo-Caribbean Feminist Thought: Genealogies, Theories, Enactments* (Palgrave Macmillan 2016) edited by Lisa Outar and Gabrielle Hosein. She previously served on the Steering Committee (Board) of Jahajee (formerly Jahajee Sisters), a gender justice organization that supports survivors of domestic abuse and sexual assault.

EDDIE BRUCE-JONES is a law professor and writer of Jamaican heritage, based at SOAS, University of London. He teaches the graduate seminar "Race, Law and Literature" alongside courses on human rights and international law. His research on the archives of indentureship in Jamaica and India has been funded by the UK's Arts and Humanities Research Council. His essays, fiction and poetry appear in *The Los Angeles Review of Books, The Feminist Review, The Huffington Post, Gasher Journal* and *Caribbean Beat*. He is essays editor at *The Offing*.

MIRANDA RACHEL DEEBRAH is a Guyanese-born writer and multidisciplinary performance artist whose works combine art and activism to increase meaningful representation and visibility for the Indo-Caribbean and Indentured Indian diasporas. She has co-directed and starred in various original South Asian/Indo-Caribbean theatrical productions in NYC, co-produced short art films with gender-justice organization Jahajee, and appeared in Lissa Deonarain's documentary film *Double Diaspora: A Portrait of Indo-Caribbeans in New York*. Miranda holds a Master's degree from Columbia University and is a licensed psychotherapist specializing in ancestral and intergenerational trauma healing for descendants of Indian Indenture.

WILL DEPOO is a writer and poet whose works delve into a wide array of themes. His writings explore themes around cuisine, gender dynamics, heritage, immigration, indentured servitude, law enforcement, and substance abuse, to name a few. Will exhibits a fondness for composing in Creolese, the language native to Guyana. Will's Guyanese heritage is deeply rooted; he resided in Guyana as a young child and learned Creolese during his stay. Moreover, he is a longstanding resident of East New York, Brooklyn. In addition to his creative pursuits, Will is a long-time organizer, dedicating his efforts to many causes. Will has organized around issues related to housing justice, tenants' rights, gender justice, criminal justice reform, and for immigrant rights. Furthermore, Will's talent as a poet has garnered recognition, with three of his poems being published in the print edition of Gasher Press's "Cherry Moon" in 2023. His unique ability to blend his cultural heritage, community organizing and poetic expression makes him a distinctive and impactful voice in the literary and social justice landscapes.

ELIZABETH JAIKARAN is a New York based author and lawyer, with work published across a spectrum of print and digital media. She began writing at the age of eight and, since then, has published fiction, non-fiction, legal commentary, poetry, and comedy. She is the child of Guyanese immigrants, born in Brooklyn, New York and raised in Queens. Her writing has appeared in the *Huffington Post*, *Playboy*, *Brown Girl Magazine*, *PREE Lit*, *Defunkt Magazine*, and *Human/ Kind Journal*. She is also the award-winning author of *Trauma: A Collection of Short Stories* (Shanti Arts 2017) and *Waiting for a Name* (Shanti Arts 2023).

SIMONE DEVI JHINGOOR is an Indo-Caribbean poet and activist based in NYC. She pens and performs poetry that speaks to her unique cultural experience as an Indo-Caribbean woman with ancestral roots in Guyana and growing up in the Bronx. Her poetry addresses themes of identity, migration, healing, and social justice issues. Simone has been a featured poet internationally and nationally at universities, spoken word venues, shows, art festivals and conferences. She has performed in the Rajkumari Cultural Center's theater productions, "Kitchrie: Festival of Indo-Caribbean Arts and Culture" in 1999,

2002 and 2009, and Jahajee Sisters' theater production, "Jahajees Rising!" in 2018. Her writing has been published in the Aerogram and in two community anthologies: "*i got something to say!*" released by Blackout Arts Collective in 2004 and "*Bolo Bahen, Speak Sister!*" released by Jahajee Sisters and Sakhi for South Asian Women in 2009. Simone has produced and curated dynamic cultural events across NYC to create a platform for artists to share their work. She has also led arts and activism programs that convene women and girls of color in spaces for creative expression, truth-sharing, and healing. Simone is currently the Co-Executive Director of Jahajee Sisters, a gender justice organization she co-founded for Indo-Caribbean women, girls and gender expansive people to heal and create lasting change by putting an end to gender-based violence.

ALIYAH KHAN is Associate Professor of Caribbean Literature in the Departments of English Language and Literature, and Afroamerican and African Studies, at the University of Michigan, Ann Arbor. She is the author of *Far from Mecca: Globalizing the Muslim Caribbean* (Rutgers University Press 2020), the first academic monograph on the history, literature, and music of Islam in the Anglophone Caribbean, including Guyana, Trinidad, and Jamaica. Dr. Khan's scholarly and creative writing also appears in venues including *GLQ, the Caribbean Review of Gender Studies, Studies in Canadian Literature, Pree: Caribbean Writing, The Rumpus,* and *Agents of Ishq*. She holds a Ph.D. in Literature and Feminist Studies from the University of California, Santa Cruz, and an M.F.A. in Fiction Writing from Hunter College of the City University of New York.

ANU LAKHAN is a writer and editor from Trinidad and Tobago. Her criticism, fiction and poetry have appeared in *Wasafiri, Bomb, Pree, Caribbean Beat* and the *Caribbean Review of Books*. Macmillan Caribbean, Explore Parts Unknown (Anthony Bourdain's web presence) and Caribbean Beat allowed her to write about food with passionate absurdity. Her work making the science of climate change accessible to lay readers is ongoing through her "Islands Like Us" series. She is the author of the chapbook *Letters to K.* And yes, she knows Kafka is dead but that doesn't stop her from trying to get in touch.

NADIA MISIR was born and raised in South Ozone Park, Queens. She is a former Asian American Writers' Workshop Open City fellow. She received her BA in English from SUNY Oswego and an MA in American studies from Columbia University. She received an MFA in writing from Queens College, CUNY, and was a Writer-in-Residence at the Louis Armstrong House Museum. Her writing has been published in *AAWW's Open City Magazine, No, Dear Mag,* and *Kweli Journal.* Follow her on Instagram @nuancednadia.

RAJIV MOHABIR is the author of *Cutlish* (Four Way Books 2021), *The Cowherd's Son* (Tupelo Press 2017, winner of the 2015 Kundiman Prize; Eric Hoffer Honorable Mention 2018) and *The Taxidermist's Cut* (Four Way Books 2016, winner of the Four Way Books Intro to Poetry Prize, Finalist for the Lambda Literary Award for Gay Poetry in 2017), and translator of *I Even Regret Night: Holi Songs of Demerara* (1916) (Kaya Press 2019) which received a PEN/Heim Translation Fund Grant Award and the 2020 Harold Morton Landon Translation Award from the American Academy of Poets. His hybrid memoir, *Antiman* (Reckless Books 2021), received the 2019 Reckless Books' New Immigrant Writing Prize. Currently he is an Assistant Professor of poetry in the MFA program at Emerson College, translations editor at Waxwing Journal and poetry editor of *Asian American Literary Review.*

KANEESHA CHERELLE PARSARD is an assistant professor in the Department of English Language and Literature at the University of Chicago. Her scholarship examines the legacies of slavery and emancipation in the Americas, and particularly concerns how gender and sexuality structure race, labor, and capital. She is currently at work on her first book project, *An Illicit Wage: Economies of Sex and the Family after West Indian Emancipation.* Her scholarship appears in *American Quarterly,* the volume *Indo-Caribbean Feminist Thought*

(2016), and *Small Axe*.

RYAN PERSADIE is an artist, educator, community organizer, and researcher based in Toronto, Canada. Currently he is pursuing a PhD in Women and Gender Studies at the Woment and Gender Studies Institute at the University of Toronto. He also carries a MA in Ethnomusicology and Sexual Diversity Studies from the University of Toronto. His aesthetic and scholarly work interrogates the relationships and entanglements between queer Indo-Caribbean diasporas, Caribbean feminisms, Afro-Asian intimacies, Ocean and Island worlds, and legacies of indenture. In particular, his work turns to sites of performance, embodiment, and popular culture as foundational archives of erotic self-making practices that work to formulate new networks, itineraries, and archipelagic routings of Indo-Caribbean feminist geographies and spatializations. Outside of academia, he organizes with the Caribbean Equality Project and as a practising drag artist where he goes by the stage name of Tifa Wine.

SUZANNE C. PERSARD is Assistant Professor of Women's, Gender and Sexuality Studies at American University. Born and raised in Bronx, New York to parents from Kingston, Jamaica, her work as an interdisciplinary scholar, writer and curator centers gender and sexuality within indentured Indian archives; queer visual culture; and historiography. She was profiled by the Smithsonian Asian Pacific American Center for her role as a founding member of Jahajee Sisters, the first organization in the United States committed to ending gender-based violence within Indo-Caribbean communities. Her academic and creative writing appear in various publications internationally. She was awarded a poetry prize from Small Axe and writing residences from Hedgebrook in Seattle and Mumbai. In 2023, she was the curator of the exhibit Remnants of Another featuring queer Indo-Caribbean visual artists at Twelve Gates in Philadelphia.

DIVYA M. PERSAUD is a planetary scientist, writer, and composer. Her forthcoming book *do not perform this: a song cycle* won the 2017 Editor's Choice Award from the 'Great' Indian Poetry

Collective, and her poems have appeared in *Anomaly, The Deaf Poets Society, The A3 Review*, and elsewhere. Her work addresses geographies of memory, performed silence, and trauma, seeking to connect generational experiences of indenture, cisheteropatriarchy, and resistance to the ground beneath and above us. She holds a Ph.D. in planetary imaging from University College London and a B.A. in geology and music composition from University of Rochester. Find her at divyampersaud.com.

NICHOLAS PETERS is a writer and human rights advocate. Nicholas applied his love of writing well into his secondary schooling and after, when he pursued his Bachelor of Arts in English – Literature & Linguistics at the University of Guyana. He began his professional life in journalism at the Kaieteur News newspaper. It was here that he was introduced to the transformative power of people and their stories. He is an awardee of the Walter Rodney Creative Writing Competition in Short Fiction for his piece *A Centuries Old Flame* where he explored Guyana's future 100 years after its independence and the arrival of oil. Nicholas is passionate about human rights development in Guyana, especially as it relates to the LGBTQI community, and Indigenous Peoples. He holds a Master of Arts in Human Rights at the University of Sussex, where he studied as a Chevening scholar. Nicholas has spent life in Guyana divided between the Demerara Coast, the Hinterland and Georgetown. These spaces have impacted how he sees the cultural and geographical diversity that is inherent to his country. For him, Guyana is an interesting experiment in what it means to be South American, Caribbean and Guyanese in a postcolonial globalised world. His writing aims to capture the intricate and connected lives that we live as we move between place, time and space.

NATASHA RAMOUTAR is an Indo-Guyanese writer by way of Scarborough (Ganatsekwyagon) at the east side of Toronto. She is the author of *Bittersweet* (Mawenzi House, 2020), a volunteer Social Media Assistant at the Festival of Literary Diversity, and the co-editor of *FEEL WAYS*, an anthology of Scarborough writing.

KRYSTAL M. RAMROOP is an innovative, first-generation Indo-Guyanese American author and actress. Besides her former work within the higher education industry, Krystal's a music, film, and tea junkie at heart, and hopes her curiosity and niche for cross-cultural writing will allow her to share her research and experiences and create a realm for readers to join her in. Her writings have been cited in academia and published online and in print for numerous literary magazines, journals, books, and Caribbean anthologies. She was also a featured guest on *The Cutlass Podcast* and *The Logistics Monk Show.*

CHANDANIE SOMWARU'S 2020 chapbook of poems *Urgent || Where The Mind Goes || Scattered* was the winner of an editor's choice award from Ghostbird Press. Her work can be found in *A Gathering Together, Asian American Writers' Workshop, No, Dear, Peach Velvet,* and more. She received her MFA in poetry from Queens College, City University of New York.

ACKNOWLEDGEMENTS

Thank you to each of the contributors of this anthology and to the anvil of the Caribbean plantation that hammered us into who we are.

Thank you to Neelanjana Banerjee, Austin Nguyen, Sunyoung Lee, and to all the people at Kaya Press who are dreaming up a better world for all of us.

Thank you to the Ajis and Ajas, the Nanis and Nanas who wove for us a new world out of the fabric of Kala Pani.

Thank you to my Aji who showed me the brilliance of our languages and songs.

Thank you to the dance that will not let us go.